The New Estonian Golden Age

How Estonia will rise to be one of Europe's
five richest nations

By Alexander Grover

D1491245

The New Estonian Golden Age
How Estonia will rise to be one of Europe's
five richest nations.

Published by Create Space, an Amazon.com company
Cover Design by: Media Menu International AS (Estonia)

ISBN 1441466398
EAN-13 9781441466396

BISAC: History/Europe/Baltic States/Estonia

Book websites:
www.estoniangoldenage.com
www.thenewestoniangoldenage.com

This book can be ordered on www.amazon.com

This book is dedicated to the Estonian people.

Eesti Uus Kuldaeg…..

Contents

Forward

This book is about the future, the decisions that have been or will be have to be made, the resulting benefits and the consequences of these decisions. This book challenges conventional thinking and paradigms to its core. It makes the obvious readily visible to all. I am attempting to encourage people to think in a different way and to question what they hold close to their hearts and believe as absolute truths so they can enjoy the life they so dearly desire.

Disappointment and surprise are two words we hear often in economic circles. Both are based on the magnitude of deviation from a prediction. Surprise is when the deviation affects us positively and disappointment is when this deviation affects us negatively. People have been making predictions about the economy but we never questioned them when we were surprised, but scorn them when we were disappointed. We barely questioned when things were going right; why we were not meeting the predictions and what would the later consequences be?

A democratic nation or tribe has three pillars to its existence: economics, politics and military. First, a nation must possess a strong and decisive leadership cadre who can effectively balance short term needs with long term vision and guide the nation and its people to prosperity. Second, a nation must have a viable economy with industries that meet both domestic and international demands for the long term. And finally, the most overlooked factor by many international investors, a nation must have the means to defend its society and bounty from aggression.

On the surface we know what went wrong and how we got here. But now we must look at building on what went right and outline the decisions that have to be made to reach "The New Estonian Golden Age". Each of these decisions has both positive and negative consequences that must be examined in detail. Estonians are great well intentioned people with warm hearts and very high levels of intellect but they are being misguided by some highly insecure and vindictive elitists. The new generation of Estonian leadership will have to be forward thinking and pragmatic while considering the history and culture of the nation. The new leaders will have to think unlike any leaders in the past and break from certain aspects of traditional thinking if they want any chance of saving the society.

Estonians must face the reality that the politicians in Brussels and Washington DC do not really consider their needs directly but more as an afterthought. After all, Estonia has only 1.3 million of the 500 million EU inhabitants and contributes only ~$29 Billion to the total $14 Trillion or ~0.2% of the total European Union economy. The European Union incorporated the Baltics to create a buffer with Russia, extend their markets and snatch talent. In return they offered only massive price inflation and a fine for excess sugar. The American spirit of self-determination must be applied: only Estonians can make the future bright for Estonia.

Estonia is on the precipice of an unprecedented economic unwinding with an incomprehensible aftermath. The actions taken now and in the future will have repercussions for many generations. There are no easy answers and no silver bullet to get out of the current situation. This mess was not created solely by the Estonian people but also by their leaders, the media and trusted foreign advisors. We must move beyond fixing the blame to fixing the problem in a real nuts and bolts way. This book presents a bold approach to the attitude adjustment that must take place so that the nation can reach bright and prosperous future that lies ahead.

Introduction:

Five years ago I remember listening to the vision
articulated by one of the nation's leaders that Estonia will
become one of the five richest nations in Europe. This
assumption was based on the unfettered continuation of the
current economic trajectory at the time. However, I never
heard the strategy and action plan that would sustain the
growth trajectory and later achieve this goal. Recently, I
read a defeatist article where the same leaders are now
stating that this dream was farfetched. I contend that this
dream is attainable but Estonians must ask themselves first
what choices must be made, second what actions must be
taken and finally consider and balance the consequences
thereof. Success comes from not only having grand vision
but also from the effectiveness in the execution of the series
of multiple tasks that make up the goal. The key issues at
stake are demographic, cultural, energy, national defense
and economic.

Just like physical matter which can be broken down into
atoms and subatomic particles, the smallest indivisible unit

of matter, a society can be broken to into its most basic units, families and individuals. As in chemistry, when protons and neutrons come together to form atoms and subsequently these atoms come together and form compounds which later contribute to the properties of a substance, men and women come together to form families and subsequently these families come together and form communities which later contribute to the culture of a nation. All of this combined movement among substance and people releases kinetic energy which catalyzes an economy.

An examination of specific matter at the atomic level offers great insight into how the material will behave. We can determine how reactive a substance is by the amount of electrons in its outer shell, by the amount of protons and electrons, by the shape of the atom etc. An up close examination of a society's individual and family values and dynamics can lend insight into how the general economy of a nation will behave. We can determine what they deem important, what are their dreams, what are their perceptions, what is their sense of logic, what is their grasp on reality, if they are long term vs. short term thinkers and so on. Some of these individuals and families are able to look forward, some squabble over trivial matters, others split apart while some aspire to overcome their circumstances. When all of these considerations are aggregated it can explain and even predict what will happen to a society.

However all matter, regardless of the characteristics, abides by a common universal laws such as gravity, physics, chemistry and mathematics. Anthropologists show that human migration is an ongoing and constant human phenomenon; we are not a static species confined to economic, political, ideological or social boundaries. In fact, no species has been as restless or innovative as mankind. Humans have invented clever ways to exist in every type of environment at all reaches of the earth. Humans no matter where they are from, what they wear or how they think are constantly on a quest to find more bountiful food sources and greater opportunity. Directly or indirectly, we are always seeking a better life.

When we apply the atomic view to Estonian society, we observe that most Estonians appear stunned by the swiftness of the current crisis. I spoke with all sorts of people on the streets of Tallinn, Riga and Vilnius back in 2006 and saw a combination of "ignorance is bliss attitude" mixed with loan based consumerism, xenophobia and a negative almost hostile attitude towards Russian reconciliation. Everyone was talking about how Estonia would reach greatness but not a single person could articulate how it would really happen. Almost all of the people I spoke with did not understand the concept of global competition and wage productivity. In speaking with literally hundreds of people, I realized there was and still is a serious mismatch of expectations. People want things but they either don't know how to get them or they don't want to overcome the barriers standing between them and their object of desire. Many believe that the EU, NATO or ignorant cash rich foreigners who fancy blondes will give it to them. Many Estonian men, who call themselves citizens, enjoy the benefits of a democracy and seek the privileges of living in a small exclusive country. However, many of them refuse to do their nine months of obligatory military service; in fact many try as hard as they can to avoid it by acting sick or coming up with some lame excuse. They cannot connect the fact that strong national defense is a tenant to a free and prosperous society. They cannot connect the fact that to get things, they must exchange something or do something in return.

There is a failure in the logic with many Estonians to equate the fact that certain actions have certain consequences, both good and bad. This lack of reason is taking a toll on the society as a whole, evidenced by the current economic situation. One of my colleagues expressed his discontent that small nations periodically have to bow to larger nations when it comes to foreign aid or military support, but what he failed to do was list the alternatives and their associated consequences. In essence there is a failure in cost benefit analysis. If Estonia goes it alone and rejects all foreign aid and its conditions then it must face another set of issues. Estonia will have complete autonomy but then it will also be deprived of the benefits of alliance and globalization. In fact every action in life like in physics is met with equal and opposite reactions. However with life, it's harder to determine what form these consequences may take.

Many Estonians have adapted the lottery ticket mentality: waiting for the one big deal where they are set for life. I have Estonian friends who have turned to online gambling and casinos as an alternate source of income instead of finding some business or service to start from their home. The consequences of the waiting for things to happen vs. the making things happen mentality is that you may miss a lot of life in the process of waiting for the big payout. Furthermore when you do hit the jackpot if it ever happens, it may be too late in life to enjoy its full benefit. The Aerosmith song called Amazing has a lyric, "Life is a journey, not a destination", that sums up the fact that we must make every day of our lives count and the fact that each small task done in sequence over a series of days should be something that gives us joy. The accomplishment of which will make the destination all the more rewarding.

Politicians stated that Estonia will one day be one of the five richest nations in Europe but then also stated that

Estonia will not be nation of immigrants like Ireland, Germany or the UK. Immigration was one of the key ingredients along with the English language that propelled Ireland, the "Celtic Tiger", out of the depths of poverty to one of the EU's five richest nations. Although Ireland's current economic state is challenged, the country has made remarkable strides and will remain a formidable EU economy. Anywhere you look in the world, true organic prosperity, immigration and diversity are inseparable. Estonia's advancement for the past 18 years was impressive; however it was just an initial and relatively easy phase: setting up defining property rights, installing basic services, starting-up initial industries, building infrastructure etc. The next phases of progress where the country steps up to the EU average are going require that Estonia competes in a globalized economy. In life it is like we can work at Mc Donald's and get the minimum wage which gives us a very basic standard of living. If we want to improve our quality of life, we need to learn new skills that differentiate us from the masses, join a leading firm and develop specific expertise which makes us invaluable to the organization. Then we can demand a higher salary since this training and experience is costly to replace.

I believe there is a failure to understand the basic concept that progress comes at the price of change and adjustment, that in order for nations to ascend, they must be willing to change with the times. The Estonian leaders and many of the people appear to want the benefits of prosperity without accepting the consequences social and demographic change.

There exists an "economic black box". Not a single person, average or affluent, has explained in detail how and what will drive any future economic recovery without some form of labor force augmentation. No one told me in concrete words: what will the primary industries be, who will the investors be, where will the workers come from and where they will live? Essentially they built a very fancy car but when one takes a closer look and examines under the hood, he will find that the engine was missing.

At the end of the day, if people are to be able to buy things, they will need money. To get this money, they will need a job. A job will be provided by a company or by the government which is funded by tax revenue collected from the people. Collectively these companies will ultimately have to provide something of value to the outside world in order for the people working in these companies to exchange their money for foreign goods not available at home. If there is a deficit of stuff to sell in comparison to what is being brought in, then the system will erode. Or in terms of physics, it will decay away. As erosion or decay takes place, the system becomes unstable and eventually collapses.

Many politicians and citizens alike believed that joining the EU was a guarantee of prosperity instead of just a beginning. There was the initial jumpstart from joining in 2004; however, there were always the lingering questions of how to keep the good times rolling. In 2006 I started to question: what it really meant in day to day terms when the Estonian kroon was strong against the dollar? I just got blank stares or this rhetoric that America was going to hell in a hand basket. At one time (euro = $1.55) it was almost 15%-20% cheaper to fly to America, buy a new Mercedes

S-Class, ship it back to Tallinn and pay the import duty and VAT than to buy it in Estonia. I get leery with such cross-border financial transactions start to encroach on The First Law of Thermodynamics. Nothing can defy financial physics for too long, disparities like this must correct back to a sensible equilibrium in one form or another, usually in a sharp manner and by surprise. This also meant in financial terms that if the upward trends in the kroon and euro persisted, it would actually be cheaper to get work done in America, when factoring in the high level of American productivity. The effects of the super strong kroon and euro anomaly would later self-correct (later in the year, the euro would plunge to the euro = $1.30 level). The Financial Times in 2008 wrote several articles about Western European companies including Volkswagen, BMW and even Airbus opting to move to the American South instead of Eastern Europe.

These conversations with locals and financial experts alike led me to the realization that the Estonian economy was being built on press releases and bullcrap by an elite group of reality challenged individuals: the President, Prime

Minister, Foreign Minister and Finance Minister to name a few. When these guys work together, the result of their combined effort is antagonism, the same kind of negative synergy you get when multiplying fractions together: $\frac{1}{2}$ x $\frac{1}{2}$ x $\frac{1}{2}$ = 1/8. Notice how the product gets smaller exponentially. This means if there is one idiot, its bad, when you put a bunch together the quality of decisions deteriorate rapidly. Subsequently I took a cautionary stance on my Baltic investments which later proved to be very profitable. I was going to refer to the leadership cadre named above as circus clowns. But then I found out that to become a clown, one must go through a rigorous selection process competitive and work a highly demanding schedule. Clowns have a respectable and enviable profession. I didn't want to offend any clowns.

Investment opportunities still exists for those willing to ask the difficult, offensive and probing questions and go the extra mile to physically examine and verify the underlying assumptions of value. Ask the obvious and most fundamental questions. There is a tendency in Estonia to analyze without asking the obvious. People obsess about statistical figures, percentages, internal rates of return etc. If the obvious can't be answered in a clear concise manner then it's probably a bad investment in the long term. Your gut instincts and street level observations of the obvious can lend more to making a proper decision about whether or not to make an investment than you may think. If you go into a restaurant and the service is slow and the staff is apathetic, then one can infer that this character goes all the way up to management.

My favorite question, in light of the low birth rate and an elevated rate of emigration among young people is, "Who will do the work". At the end of every economy is a layer of people, which is eroding in the Baltics. This means fewer consumers every year leading to a myriad of other effects. According to Baltic Times, the demographic pinch is being felt at Tartu University which expects dropping enrollments attributed to declining birth rates to drastically affect the viability of the university and the town itself.

Finding honest, transparent people who have a passion for business should be the focus of investors. All companies, investments and opportunities are only as good as the people that hold them up. Today's Baltic investors will need to form strategic alliances with local people of the highest integrity that have the courage to tell them immediately when something is going awry. Furthermore, every investment requires very strict disciplines on purchase and exit price. Currently the long term outlook remains clouded, however those who devote their time and resources can still find favorable returns. But beware, the easy money is gone.

Leadership

Democracy is alive and well in Estonia. People do have power of the vote and they will soon be able to do so by sms. The destiny and well being of so many are decided by a few entrusted elected officials. We elect people with the expectation that not only can they carry out our wishes but also make us aware of the consequences of these wishes. All over the world we rarely see the latter in our elected officials but this is what's more than needed in Estonia. The Estonian people, especially the ones living outside Tallinn (~70% of the population), should hold their leaders accountable with their votes. People need to complain less and make it known that they will vote more critically. This can change things!

Initially, Estonia was an exciting and attractive place for investors because they were bucking the general European paradigms by adapting ideas which appeared to be quite radical yet very pragmatic in terms of promoting business, enterprise and innovation. Many of the ideas appeared American in nature but were never implemented in the

USA: flat tax, free ubiquitous wireless internet coverage, streamlined banking and the ease of opening a business. Estonia is one of the easiest countries in which to incorporate a company. You can get a card reader for about $20 that connects to your laptop via USB. Just insert your ID card, from over the internet and the comfort of your own home; you can have a corporation up and running in less than a half hour.

I remember getting an information packet from the Estonian Embassy called *The Little Country that Could* which was written with the most optimistic and open views. We saw a small nation that wanted to be different, more American rather than European in nature, but then somewhere during this revolutionary path the underlying paradigm got derailed. The decision makers started to fall prey to Continental European ideals when faced with the dilemma of immigration, integration of the foreign born population, historical reflection, labour market flexibility and social welfare.

Decisiveness is an important attribute to leadership. Nothing can move unless decisions are made. It has two components: first is the ability to make a decision within a given time constraint and second is the quality of the decision itself. In the US Navy we learned that first one must just get in the habit of making decision when asked to do so, good or bad. The philosophy is that with education, time and experience, the quality of decisions will improve. I found this to be generally true and it also requires one to be willing to take counsel from experts and ask questions to ascertain the situation in order to avoid a fatal error. In most real world situations, we are given limited information and expected to make decisions. This lack of information and the corresponding inferences we make to get a better idea of the outcomes amounts to risk analysis. Decisions are sometimes about choosing between the better of two or more options. But more often, it is about choosing the least of the bad options, "picking your pain". A classic example which will be explored in detail later in this book is coal energy vs. nuclear energy. Both offer energy and both pollute, but in different ways. When making important decisions, the consequence is that there will always be an unsatisfied group of people. Choosing the least of the worst decision that strikes the balance between public opinion and getting things done is very difficult at best. The ability to trade-off short term pain for long term gain or give certain concessions for the greater overall good defines the success of politicians, businessmen and even individuals. Remember that no decision is a decision in itself: to let things continue as they are or accept the status quo. One can also argue that being neutral means favoring indirectly the side that is already in control.

There appears to be a lack of government willingness and leadership to say what needs to be said and do what needs to be done to revolutionize Estonia into one of the world's great economic powers which will create more opportunities for its general citizenry. There is a general lack of decisiveness. Leaders are stuck in committee and unwilling to make decisions and even more take no responsibility for them. As things stand, the politicians with aid of the media appear to be fixing the blame instead of the problem and they are further reinforcing self-defeating attitudes regarding the creation of a national vision. I always wondered if the politicians gave both points of view to the general population and the middle class who live in the villages throughout Estonia, in regards to immigration and reconciling with Russia. I am quite sure they only presented the negative aspects of both.

In an American Chamber of Commerce luncheon in 2008, the Estonian Foreign Minister when discussing his view on immigration was only speaking in the negative: stating the crime percentages in Helsinki attributed to Somali migrants. He failed to mention any positive stories about immigrants such as the foreign chefs in Estonia. He further failed to mention that it may be the Scandinavian system that is the problem, not the Somalis. Benny Carlson, a Swedish economic historian, recently compared the experiences of Somali immigrants in Sweden with those of Somali immigrants in Minneapolis, Minnesota (USA). Only 30 percent had a job in Sweden whereas around 60% had a job in Minneapolis. Moreover, there are about 800 businesses run by Somalis in Minneapolis, compared to only 38 in Sweden. Carlson quoted two immigrants who together summed up the disparity. "There are opportunities here", said Jamal Hashi, who runs a restaurant in Minneapolis. His friend, who migrated to Sweden instead, told a different story: "You feel like a fly trapped under a glass. Your dreams are shattered."

Ten years ago when I was living in Sweden, I had a firsthand view of this phenomenon. The Swedish government is willing to give a lot of aid to the new arrivals but they are afforded limited opportunities to rise. They are given language courses and an apartment but the law does not have Equal Employment Opportunity (EEO) where it's forbidden to discriminate on the basis of race, gender, birthplace, religion etc. Many Persians living in Sweden have changed their surnames to "Gustafson" to get better consideration for jobs. In Europe many employers require a photograph on the CV which is forbidden in the USA. The "Jantelagen" is used socially to restrain immigrants from having the aspiration to walk as equals with the indigenous members of the population (Google: Jantelagen, it lends a lot of insight into Scandinavian mentality). In a way, they are given support but told to know their place and given a clear message they never will truly be Swedish. I recall meeting a Swede of Turkish origin who, along with other Swedes, told me, "he really isn't Swedish". I was really dumbfounded. He was born in Sweden, spoke the language fluently, did his compulsory army time, had a job as a subway driver and paid those high taxes. It took me some time to figure out that being Swedish was about genetics and not by birth or by contribution to society.

Politicians continue to ramble about the negative aspects of Russia but failed to mention that much of the current infrastructure and many of the buildings we live in were built by the Soviets. Additionally, most of the Estonians of Russian descent work and pay taxes without incident. This single sided rhetoric on key issues has cheated most Estonians out of an opportunity to pursue a better life and has placed the Estonian nation's existence into deeper peril. The leaders took the easy way out by uniting people with hate: finding a boogey man to blame for all the problems instead of uniting the nation on consensus and cross-cultural understanding. The people in media, politics, diplomatic core and business who hold positions of power have an obligation to give the average Estonian a balanced picture when the channels of information are fairly limited, a fact characteristic to any young nation.

My observations during conversation are that many highly intelligent and capable Estonians appear to suffer from "analysis paralysis". I also notice many of them in the business world lack the basic self-confidence to go out in the world and compete head to head with their Western peers, when in many cases they are actually capable to not only compete but also win. They will defeat themselves on just about every subject with complex mathematical and statistical analysis. This is the result of insecure journalist, leaders and teachers who fail to understand the potential of the future which is in our control is far more important than the problems of the past which can not be changed. There exists irresponsibility in the media who feeds on the general population's lack of knowledge and emotions to sensationalize the news to fit an agenda. One must wonder why the Estonian leadership and intellectuals can't build from the triumph and mistakes of others. Perhaps they are incompetent and spread propaganda to consolidate their power because if people knew better; their positions would be challenged, putting them out of work.

Estonians should really question how much their politicians love their country and care about future prosperity of each individual. Some of the current leaders are even Soviet era holdovers. Former President Arnold Rüütel was the president of Estonia from 2001-2006. He was also served as also served as the last Chairman of the Supreme Soviet of the Estonian SSR from March 29, 1990 to October 6, 1992. He received the Order of Lenin in 1971 and The Order of the Badge of Honor in 1964. The current prime minister of Estonia Andrus Ansip was also the Communist Party's organizational head in Tartu in the 1980's. He is constantly fighting allegations that he used force including tear gas and dogs against his own people during Soviet times. While I was in high school during the Reagan era, the prevailing motto was, "once a communist, always a communist."

Estonian politicians at all levels have been involved bribery and corruption scandals, sometimes ones that favor enemies of the state. Case in point: the spy scandal of Herman Simm, an Estonian defense ministry official with Estonian and NATO clearance, disclosed state and NATO secrets to the Russians. The Bronze Nights of April 2007 (the riots in connection with the relocation of the Soviet Bronze Statue) raise some interesting questions when considering the background of the current Prime Minister. The former communist, who may have used force against his own people, made a very public and antagonistic campaign to remove the Bronze Soldier. It is quite suspicious when considering that Ansip and Putin both were both dealing with popularity issues and questions about their leadership at the time. Putin's party and their favored project, the port of Ust-Luga project in St. Petersburg, were facing challenges. Ust-Luga was a very expensive (~$2.1B) endeavor that was supposed to serve as an alternative to Baltic shipping ports. However, at the time, most Russian enterprises preferred to ship through Estonia due to its low cost and relative efficiency. Why fix what isn't broke? The Bronze Statue was a rallying point for both Russians and Estonians who were equally passionate but on opposite sides of the issue. The ensuing riots where around 1000 were arrested, dozens injured and one killed made both leaders extremely popular among their people. Both leaders could focus the attention away from internal problems to the "hostile neighboring country. The Russians were calling the Estonians fascists and the Estonians were accusing the Russians of aggression. Ansip's approval soared in the polls and in March 2008 Putin was able to get his protégé, Dmitry Medvedev, elected as Prime Minister. Putin stayed involved as the Russian President. Ust-Luga was opened by Putin himself in May 2008. At the same time, the profits from the transit business through Estonian ports declined by over 40% according to Estonian government statistics. The organizers of the riots were recently acquitted of all charges by the county court and now we see both countries starting dialog at the state level.

In the United States, Robert Hanssen was a senior FBI (Federal Bureau of Investigation) agent who spied for the Soviet Union and Russia for more than 20 years. He was finally caught in 2001 while attempting to trade state secrets for money near his home. He revealed some of the most classified projects in the United States including a tunnel going under the Russian Embassy in Washington DC and names of double agents. The KGB and FSB are highly regarded for their ability to recruit spies at the very highest levels of government, military and industrial entities to serve the long term interests of the Russian Federation.

"A democratic society depends upon an informed and educated citizenry" (Thomas Jefferson). The ability of the current cadre of politicians to lead and educate shows in the latest economic numbers. They have managed to manipulate the common population to choose continued poverty and into believing being poor is the only way to keep Estonian culture intact. Furthermore, this reapplication of Soviet style propaganda has created an isolationist attitude which uniquely combines a grand sense of entitlement mixed with a national inferiority complex. This has fueled a consumption boom in the bling-bling sector with the attitude that someone else will pay for it later. There was a massive proliferation in sms (short term – high interest) loans that were charging, in come cases, up to 1000% interest. Tallinn also became famous for being a party city (The New York Times declared Tallinn the best party city in 2006) with one of the highest per capita Hummer ownership rates. The book Hard Landing (hardlanding.ee) written by Claudio Zucchelli and Dag Kirsebom chronicles the Estonian age of decadence further.

The new breed of Estonian leader will have to be raging bulls, people with a background in team sports like Mart Poom or Estonian Army officers who served in combat. They will understand the sheer power of human will, determination, self-confidence, endurance, guts and the fact that every person no matter where they are from are pretty much the same regardless of race, culture and ethnicity. Estonians need to elect winners to move ahead. Winners understand the sacrifices required to win in battle, win on the playing field, bring home the gold medals or build a great nation. Winners will not propagate their insecurities over a society; instead they will use reason and logic to make people aware of all options. They will advocate those choices which may be painful in the short term but ensure survival in the long term. But more so they will frame these choices, dilemmas and conundrums in such a way the average person can comprehend the consequences of each decision. Winners consider emotions but are not driven by them. Winners are secure people who want to share their success by creating opportunity for others and recognize the need for opposition and diversity to further strengthen their position. They always ask what is next, how can we be better, go higher, leap further etc. Estonians more than ever need leaders with strength of character, decisive nature and courage.

Current State and Future Trajectory

Currently, the economy is converging more than declining. The Estonian GDP is about 75% of the EU average. In the USA, a union that has been around for almost 300 years, the bottom states, Arkansas, Mississippi and West Virginia, are around 55%-70% of convergence when compared to the US average and have been so for many decades. Thus we can conclude that Estonia is well in the convergence zone and the current policies will only allow future expected growth rates to be marginal at best and mostly in line with overall European growth.

Convergence in of itself is an interesting concept with everything based on per capita statistics. What is remarkable about these fractional based statistics is that the number grows in two ways: either by increasing the numerator or by decreasing the denominator, which in this case is the population. According to Estonian Government statistics, the population of Estonia in 1989 was over 1.5 million and in 2007 it was around 1,342,409 with the current rate of depopulation at ca. -0.632% and migration of -3.2 migrant(s)/1,000 population (2006 est.). The Estonian government recently released a report that births exceeded deaths. People misinterpret this data to mean positive population growth. However this fact says nothing of actual population growth and it fails to take into account migration rates. Moreover, this trend has to be maintained to be meaningful.

The "capita erosion", i.e. depopulation, will on paper make Estonia look quite ok. Square meters per capita will grow, autos per capita will grow, shopping centers per capita, mobiles per capita, internet per capita etc will all rise, but not in the way investors would hope for. The losses of people will not lead wealth redistribution to the masses. The GDP per capita may look good but the distortion of wealth distribution will continue to grow.

As the saying goes, the rich will get richer and poor will get poorer. Currently in Estonia, one must have contacts and connections to make big things happen. As the economy shrinks, fewer companies will start to control greater market share in a shrinking market. In essence, they will have limited long term growth prospects as the pool of potential customers shrinks every year. This will push nepotism and cronyism among the elite to an even higher level than it is now. The average Estonian will have very limited opportunity to advance and make a better life. Many people will inherit multiple flats, increasing per capital living space, but there will be no one to sell them too. Moreover, there will be limited money to renovate them. Thus we can expect to see most real estate prices continue downward. This new found misery will most likely have negative impact on the birthrate, further exacerbating the demographic retreat. It is quite unpredictable how depopulation will play out and this uncertainty creates a lot of risk.

If Estonian leadership and mentality remains on the current vector, we should expect the unemployed well educated masses of young people to gradually emigrate westward and a rise in social ills such as alcoholism along with the depression associated with diminished hopes of wealth and prosperity. Depopulation and especially the exodus of young women mean fewer mobile phone subscriptions, fewer customers to purchase clothing, fewer families to purchase fuel, electricity and gas and so on. Estonian and European companies in general will have to cover costs with a smaller pool of customers. This will affect profitability and later negatively affect stock prices. The migrants are usually the young, smart, driven and ambitious types whose character and skills would disproportionally contribute to domestic economic production. Estonia does not have to worry about massive unemployment as much as the effects of emigration which will limit the capacity for any future economic growth.

Considering the above, it should be no surprise that asset values and stock prices are in decline and are now generally lower than before the boom started in 2004. The assumptions for valuations and growth potential must be called into question and rebased on the assumption that the customer base will recede over the long term. Corporate large scale capital investment decisions to build durable goods factories, power plants, etc generally consider timelines in the order ten or more years (typical GAAP deprecation for factory facilities is around 20-30 years).

Western nations such as Germany, UK, Ireland and especially Canada are still offering positions for skilled young people with drive, especially in nursing and IT. There are still many more positions for those willing to do "dirty jobs" (oil field workers, fisherman, butchers, clean-up, etc). Perhaps there were tens of millions of openings years ago, but now they may just have a few million for the same type of positions. If Estonia ends up with 10% unemployment which is around 100,000 people in real numbers and if just 35,000 of these newly available people spread throughout the EU, UK, Switzerland, Norway Japan, Dubai, Canada and the USA, then we are back to relatively low unemployment and perhaps another labor shortage, one of the factors precipitating the current crisis. It is ludicrous to think that people will be so easily willing to notch down their lives to save the CEO's lifestyle. In theory the so called productivity will rise, however the reality is quite different. People will not work more for less; they will drink more and work less enthusiastically. Every free moment they have they will be distracted with anxiety and job hunting efforts. History has shown that when long periods of hardship are bestowed upon a society, although reluctant at first, the inhabitants will migrate to places of greater opportunity and hope. In physics and chemistry this is known as diffusion. We should be aware than even in the current crisis, the Estonian workforce is highly leveraged!

I personally witnessed a phenomenon called "Facebook Emigration": young girls use their intelligence and communication skills on social networking sites to hook guys and marry their way out of Estonia to places such as Silicon Valley, Miami, Norway and other western destinations where their natural beauty is much appreciated and in some cases highly profitable. Their children and subsequent grand children are less and less likely to keep their Estonian heritage. As humorous as this may sound, this anecdote highlights the fact that the gifted youth who could provide domestic leadership and an intellectual workforce are using their brains and in many cases their good looks to go westward where they can climb their way up to self-actualization.

The American or European Way

The Europeans have an excellent knowledge of history, culture and the arts which they unfortunately use to hold grudges and as ammunition when bickering among themselves about past history. Some of the best examples of Continental European cultural conflicts are in the former Yugoslavia, Northern Ireland, Vlad the impaler (aka count Dracula) in Romania, Greeks and Turks, Armenians vs. Turks, Basque separatists in Spain and so on.

Tragically, Europeans are falling back to their old ways during these economic times while Americans progress through the race issue and start to challenge other ideological barriers. According to the latest Pew Survey of Global Attitudes, Anti Semitism is on the rise in continental Europe and Russia. According to the survey released in 2008, anti-Semitism has more than doubled in Spain over the past three years, rising from 21% to 46%, the survey of almost 25,000 people across 24 countries found, while more than one in three Poles and Russians also had unfavorable opinions of Jews. In the same period anti-

Semitism also rose from 21% to 25% in Germany and from 12% to 20% in France among those saying they had unfavorable opinions of Jews. The unfavorable opinion of Jews in the US and UK has been stable and low for several years at between 7 and 9%. While the Continental Europeans are looking to fix the blame, the Americans are looking to fix their leadership who will in turn fix the problem. The last time a European nation (Germany) pursued the anti-Semitic track, the results were quite disastrous. [1]

Muslims in America, even after the 9-11 attacks are afforded the full rights and protections of the US Constitution whereas in France and Turkey, the wearing of headscarves have been limited by legislation. These types of anti-Islamic laws will only make the fundamentalists stronger as they alienate segments of the society. In the United States even Nazis and Communists are free to express themselves. Ironically support for both of the above is stronger in Europe where their expression is curtailed. Freedom of expression applies to every person all the time. Tolerance is a virtue and the ability to allow all groups to peacefully express themselves signifies significant strength within a society.

Nationality has two paradigms: ideological and genetic. The people of the new world (North and South America) believe that their nations culture can be acquired by simply living in the place and going through a rite of passage to become equals with the current citizens. The old world, mostly continental Europe believes that nationality and culture is genetic. They believe that a person must be born into the culture, have a certain look, speak a certain language and possess a specific DNA composition to be considered a member of the nation. Currently, any foreigner who enters Estonia, learns the language, pays the taxes and even does military service is still regarded as a foreigner among the average citizenry. This social acceptance dilemma is also true of all other continental European nations. This notion of genetic based nationality is flawed and it is the root cause of social unrest, genocide and ethnic cleansings throughout European history. America had strong governmental forces and well organized movements among the people to continuously perfect the application Abraham Lincoln's words, "all men are created equal". It took more than 100 years for the USA to reach this point where people are for the most part judged on merit. I always wonder why Estonia wants to reinvent the ideological wheel which took hundreds of years to perfect when the history lesson is readily available. The application of which will save the current and future generations much unnecessary toil.

There was a time when Europe was more advanced than the USA in social integration. Blacks were free in Europe many generations before the Americas. I always wondered why European institutions never took the next steps to include the minorities into the national identity. In the Baltics, King Gedeminos built Vilnius by inviting people from diverse backgrounds to take part in the construction of the new Lithuanian capital city. Later these immigrants would live as equals among its native inhabitants. Lithuania was a proud and diverse society; while at the top of its existence around 1430, the Great-Duchy of Lithuania bordered the Black Sea and was one of the largest nations in Europe. Even before America was founded, Europe was on a progressive and inclusive track. In fact, much of the reason the northern states emancipated the slaves during the Civil War was to gain ideological favor with European nations who were considering an alliance with the Confederacy.

It has been scientifically proven by iGENEA (the renowned Swiss Institute for Genetic Research, administered by Gentest.ch GmbH) that the physiological difference between an Estonian and all other nationalities or ethnic groups is almost non-existent; DNA is identical to a degree of 99.9% for all people. The remaining 0.1% is the source of individual differences (such as eye colour, certain risks of disease, or deviations with no apparent function). If Estonian genetics were so different, they would be their own species and only Estonians could have children with other Estonians. But in fact we see much mixture around Tallinn: African, Russian, Indian, Italian, British, Korean, Japanese and Scandinavian mixing with Estonians. Many of those children that I met have reached adulthood with the same or stronger confidence and determination than their "pure" counterparts. It is interesting to know that pure gold in itself is quite beautiful but nonetheless too weak for jewelry or industrial use. It must be alloyed or mixed with small amounts of tin or other metals to make it strong enough for practical use. In chemistry as in society a certain amount of diversity is needed to move forward. Nazi Germany's defeat by the allies should be a lesson that the race purity argument is bogus and there is no such thing as a master race.

There are crucial differences between patriotism and nationalism. According to a US Journalist, Sydney J. Harris, "The difference between patriotism and nationalism is that the patriot is proud of his country for what it does, and the nationalist is proud of his country no matter what it does." I contend not only do patriots constantly question the actions of their government but also they take pride in the fact anyone can join their country and contribute to the continuous change for the greater good. Patriots believe dissent helps strengthen the national character and further helps the nation evolve to meet changing demands. Nationalists believe anyone with a dissenting opinion is a threat to the nation when in fact dissent only threatens the ruling faction. Nationalist feel threatened by diversity as it creates new challenges whereas Patriots feel diversity brings new ideas and creates new opportunities. Nationalists want to create a society cloned from an ideal whereas patriots believe that the combination of ideas creates the ideal environment for a society.

Being patriotic and inclusive appears to have been and still remains a better track to not only survival but also prosperity. American states if compared to European nations are by far much wealthier (See Appendix 1). Americans enjoy on average a much higher standard of living, more social mobility, consumer choice and flexibility with their lives[2]. American physcology embraces maverick behavior, defying the odds, overcoming adversity, transparency and always looking for a new challenge whereas European physcology embraces remaining in the middle, following the rules, creating ambiguity and being pedantic.

The US Constitution was written over 220 years ago by men who didn't trust government. They had just waged a revolution against the King of England. To the founders of the new republic, strong government meant autocracy. So they set up a system with an elaborate separation of powers to ensure a weak government. Hence, the secret of American government is that it was designed not to work very well. However, when compared to the EU during a time of crisis, it's an enviable model of efficiency. The EU constitution created in the 21st century was over 400 pages whereas the US constitution, adopted in 1787, along with the Bill of rights and its amendments is only 17 pages! This highlights the historical inability of European nations to set aside petty differences and to agree on basic tenants for the greater good.

This may sound like American cheerleading but no one can dispute the facts. Many Europeans contend America's success is just luck or mixing, that America is not a real nation. However, with these arguments, neither is Brazil, Mexico, Argentina or Canada which are also formable global economic players. I personally find that many Europeans are highly educated and intelligent people but their logic and ability to reason is not congruent to basic mathematics and the forces of nature. In one way I feel that American logic is designed to adjust to the ever changing global environment whereas European logic expects the global environment to adjust to them.

There are many great lessons in American history that could be applied to the problems plaguing Estonia today. History along with its successes and errors has a habit of repeating itself over and over again. America was, at one time, thirteen separate colonies under the British monarchy's thumb. They not only had different languages, religions, cultures and currencies but also very different views regarding issues such as slavery, trade, role of government, taxation, and the Native Americans. An even earlier example of unification for survival and the greater good can be found in Ancient Greece: Greek city states such as Athens Sparta, Thebes, Molossia, Corinth, Argos and Macedonia united together to fight common threats long before the time of Christ.

The American Constitution was a miracle in that so many leaders from diverse backgrounds with varied self-interests were not only able to pull it together against Britain (the reigning superpower of the time) but also hold this relatively unstable mass of colonies together and continue to grow and solidify it into a nation. There were tragedies such as the Civil War, slavery and injustice such as the "Trail of Tears" and segregation. Although cohesion was never smooth process, America and its inhabitants continued to reconcile and move on. The common theme is that united we stand – divided we fall. Together we can achieve more. There are generally more similarities than differences between people. This was all achieved before the onset of mobile phones, sms and email.

The disparity between the old and new world thinking is further evidenced statistically by the culture of innovation in the USA: Americans who are around 4% of the world's population have created more patents, which equate to new ideas, than all other nations combined [3]. The United States also has clear dominance in winning Nobel Prizes despite our social and educational problems. Furthermore, the average birthrate in the USA is 2.10, much higher than and more sustainable (The USA is the only industrial country with a positive birthrate!) than the European average of 1.50 which is leading to negative population growth [4]. America is easier to predict than Europe in terms of what will happen in the next 30 to 50 years. Looking ahead, it's hard to predict how this depopulation and general animosity towards immigrants will rear itself in Europe. Some academics have even predicted that Europe will become another Islamic state; others predict Germany, Spain and UK will be the winners at the expense of others. On the other hand, America has throughout its history righted its wrongs, led the world in breakthrough innovations, been able to ward off strategic threats and continued to grow its population.

American history shows a constant evolution where values remained relatively constant but the cultural interpretation of those values has changed for the better. America is a responsive nation on a constant quest to self-analyze and correct itself for the better. The same constitution has allowed for the abolition of slavery and segregation and brought about continuous challenge and debate leading to ongoing progress. The nature of the American system is for individuals to develop inner strength and constantly challenge the status quo whereas the European system encourages people to conform and to uphold arcane traditions without question.

Estonians should question what is so great about being European; they are better off being mavericks and finding their own way. The idea is to take lessons from America without becoming American. Ironically, that is the true American way; incorporate the lesson learned from the mistakes along with triumphs of others. Then progress forward while retaining your own identity.

Dealing with History and Ensuring Survival

"Holding a grudge is like drinking poison and waiting for the other person to die" (Carrie Fischer). The first thing Estonia must to achieve greatness is to forgive the trespasses of Soviet occupation. The best way to deal with the past is to simply let it go since you can't change it anyway. We must understand that the USSR was the "evil empire" – deemed by the late President Ronald Reagan and many Russians have suffered along with Eastern Europeans, Afghans and countless others [5]. As hard as it may be, forgiveness is the only way to move forward. I am not sure how long people want to wait for prosperity. The current party line which states that a whole generation must pass for healing to complete will take 40-50 years. Estonians need to ask themselves if they want to *wait till their dead* to enjoy prosperity. Currently, Estonian leadership is doing something unique with their history: they using it to institutionalize animosity towards their own indigenous Russian population and Russia to ensure another generation end up with a lack of self-confidence, spirit of self-determination and uncompetitive in the global economy.

50

This useless bantering is nothing more than an obvious ploy to get votes. It really does not solve any problems nor does it lead the country down the path to riches.

A great example of the power of forgiveness after massive bloodshed can be found in post American Civil War history. Abraham Lincoln, the sixteenth US president, led the country during and after the Civil War. Around 620,000 Americans died, North and South alike, from 1861-1865. However, instead of placing the Confederate president and top general (Jefferson Davis and Robert E. Lee) on trial, they were forgiven along with all Southerners. Lincoln wrote, "malice towards none; but charity for all" in a memoir dating back to the late 1860's. It emphasized that for the nation to heal and move on, the people must come together and move forward. Reconstruction was difficult at best and many differences persisted between North and South for generations later. However, the shift in attitude made all the difference and kept the US from imploding.

"Life is 10% what happens and 90% how you react to it" quoted by Charles R. Swindoll sums up the fact that we all have options on how we react to our circumstances. Choose one option and your free from the demons of the past; choose the other and the next generation can be as troubled as this current one. Estonia can learn from the past mistakes of others and build on the current success stories of others and rise from history or it can keep fomenting this current attitude and further delay any chance of prosperity into the next century. If Estonia is going to make its mark in the global economy during this generation, they will have to reconcile with the Russians and accept their own indigenous Russians with open arms as equals.

Imagine where Estonia would have been today if the leadership followed Lincoln's post civil war example, having the divine power to forgive back in 1991. The power of forgiveness and reconciliation may have enabled a whole generation to have grown up with a sense of joy, high self-esteem and self confidence. Most Estonians would have been competitive by western standards and able lead in multicultural environments. Right now only a few Estonians, mostly those who are highly educated and those with privileged lineage, enjoy this luxury which is taken for granted by the most average of western people. Estonians, the government and media must rise above the prevailing victim mentality which allows them to make excuses for non-performance, and look forward with a love for all – kick some ass attitude.

Immigration and Demographics

"Estonian Nokia" is the dream of an Estonian based multinational company with global reach and notoriety which will, in turn, bring about a wealthy society. Nokia is an amazing Finnish high tech company most recognized around the world for its technologically advanced yet artistically designed GSM handsets. They pioneered the idea that the mobile phone is more than a communication tool; that it is also a means of personal expression. Nokia achieved this success in a field that moves at light speed by being adaptable and able to recognize they need the best talent bar-none. Nokia embraces the long proven ideal that diversity creates value and innovation. Nokia leadership and engineering is made up of some of the best people which were recruited from all corners of the planet. Nokia managed to trump much larger rivals such as Motorola and Ericsson. This was supported and made possible by Finland's responsive immigration policy, recognition that talent is not exclusive to any one group of people and the best ideas are created by a combination of talents and backgrounds.

The multicultural society concept was born out of the New World but mostly emphasized and institutionalized in the USA. Although there was slavery and segregation, the efforts of government have reconciled this tragic past and America is now truly and equal opportunity society which embraces its entire people, evidenced by the election of Barack Obama. Many American leaders such as Bill Clinton and Senator Robert Byrd transformed from bigotry to champions of civil rights within their own lifetime. This was all possible because of the media and leadership taking a bold and revolutionary stance. They understood that change is necessary for progress to occur and realized their own views were wrong and did not wish it upon their children. They US system is still far from perfect but there is continual effort to give people of all backgrounds equal opportunity and equal access to education and resources to better themselves.

Estonians must embrace immigration if they want to realize this dream to be among the five richest nations in Europe. Estonia can build a society based on immigration without losing the basics of its culture such as language, food and traditions. This can be achieved by creating laws that are open, productive and realistic. I propose the following provisions: First, English should be introduced as a second official language so that the country will be more competitive in the global economy by increasing its ability to attract skilled workforce. Second, people who were born in Estonia should be waived from the language requirement and granted citizenship. Russian can be made into a recognized language to ease the pain of transition. This is just the right thing to do. Older people already have many obligations and it is difficult for them to learn. Statelessness among working and family age people will just further fuel the anxiety and animosity within the nation. Third, any new immigrants under 33, their existing children and future offspring will have to learn Estonian to gain citizenship. Those immigrants under 29 will also have to do two years of public service in the form of part-time teaching, nursing, medicine or military duty. This way the society can heal its past, function and grow economically while building a base of Estonian-literate people for the next generation.

The increased tax base resulting from the change in policy can be used to fund the schools, cultural and language programs and national defense. Furthermore, native Estonian birthrates should increase as the economy and optimism increase. It's chess more than a checkers game to continue the culture. In the short term you may have to give up a little and accept things out of you realm of understanding but in the long term you get a society that will be the envy of the world. Remember, Estonia can trump the Americans in addition to the Europeans. The goal is not to converge but to be number one.

The European model of immigration never allowed for true ubiquitous assimilation and thus the immigrants are less motivated and unable to adapt the local culture and help build the society. This also may explain why Europe is unable to innovate at the rate of the United States. This culture of innovation can only be achieved by embracing the value of diversity. Silicon Valley with a population of around three million people, leads the world in innovation with companies like Apple, Dell, Cisco, Google and Yahoo. Many of these examples were started in a garage or dorm room with just a few bucks and a dream. Silicon Valley makes up one percent of the US population but filed 11 percent of the US patents and received over 25% of all the venture capital invested in the United States according to a survey by Silicon Valley Network in 2006. This non profit group's demographic data illustrated that the valley is 40% white, 33% Asian and 38% is foreign born who also account for 53% of valley's working engineers and scientists. This leads one to conclude that the Silicon Valleys spirit of innovation and enterprise is inseparable from the presence of immigrants.

The other major difference between European and American immigration is the support given to new arrivals by the government. This is a counterintuitive concept. When people arrive to the USA, the amount of government support is extremely limited; however, the opportunities are unlimited. Furthermore the government through legislation gives immigrants total equality (the only exception being foreign born can't run be president). In Europe, especially in Scandinavia, we find that governments give generous amounts of aid in the form of language lessons, apartments and monthly stipends but they are never included or treated as equals by the indigenous members of the society.

For immigration to truly succeed, a leap in mentality must occur. Estonians must acknowledge that the immigrants will be their equals as well as their employees and even their managers. They have as much to learn from the immigrants as the immigrants have to learn from them. Estonians must value the merit and ability the instead of genetics and appearances of an individual. The children of immigrants will be taking part in politics and have the opportunity to rise to the highest levels of political office. This American approach to immigration will not only draw the best and the brightest but also the most spirited and determined. Estonia can be a land of dreams and hope instead of being a place of exodus.

With bold implementation, then Estonia can find itself a rich and highly educated country with the lives of everyday middle-class people improving substantially. Immigration itself will create economic demand. The new arrivals will need housing, furniture, consumer goods etc. They will pay taxes which the revenues can be used to further develop the countries infrastructure, cultural institutions and defense. The immigrants, if they feel they belong and are accepted by the society, will be the greatest contributors and bring many new ideas which can be blended with old traditions to spark a wave of unprecedented innovation.

Economic Engines

The Estonian economy needs a true economic engine. In essence, a driving force that generates revenue with immunity to economic cycles. This industry needs to be a world class and always striving to be on the cutting edge. In the past the economy was mainly built by selling assets to foreigners, primarily real estate. There is a limited amount of manufacturing and logistics; however, no nation gets rich unless it steps up from being a sector follower to an innovation leader.

Right now, the Estonian economy is a "black box". As before mentioned, no one has described in detail an industry that generates <u>sustainable</u> revenue aside from the tourism industry, which is not enough to make the nation wealthy. I had a colleague tell me that EU structural funds were a source of income. I equate this idea to a kid who gets an allowance from his parents. He may be comfortable but he will never get rich and always be at the mercy of his parents. When the kid turns 18, he will stop getting this allowance and he will have to fend for himself. Estonians have to look beyond what equates to begging the European Union for funds to developing an industries that foster steady and solid growth. Estonia's European Union structural funds are slated to end in 2013. So now is the time to get it together.

When I posed the question "what will people actually do", the answer I got ranged from silly to ridiculous. My favorite two answers from highly intelligent people were, "before Soviet times, Estonia was richer than Finland" or "there never was a Protestant country that was poor". My answers to these questions are simply, Finland was not rich in pre-war times and there is always a first time for everything. Estonia must press further and aspire to find an economic engine or everything will grind to a halt when foreign investors wise up and find that the black box is in fact actually empty.

If Estonians want to see their lives improve immediately, English should be adopted as the second official language under the before mentioned provisions. This will lower the bureaucratic hurdles faced by foreign owned businesses. In turn, this will lead to more jobs for Estonians and more tax revenue for the government. It's unreasonable to want economic prosperity and expect to foreigners, especially investors who bring in money, to learn a new language while trying to operate their businesses and get situated in a land far away from their home. Estonians need to understand investors have many choices and they must make their choice more attractive than the alternatives. Furthermore, English as a second official language will give businessmen working in the service sector more flexibility in hiring. For example, labor shortages in the hotel sector were so bad that it delayed some openings by up to six months, costing millions of Euros. Believe it or not, being able to hire English speaking foreigners in the service sector will lead to more jobs for everyone in the long term. The businesses will be able to serve more clients and earn more money which will find its way into the economy and in turn create more opportunities. Also these foreign employees' earnings will find its way into the local economy creating more opportunities for local entrepreneurs. Already Singapore and Hong Kong, small but rapidly rising economies, use English as a second language. They realize English is the de-facto global language. If a Russian, Dane and Brazilian have a meeting, they will mostly likely default to English.

Estonia may want to also consider adapting Russian as a recognized working language since ca. 30% of the population is ethnic Russian and it is on the cross-roads of Europe and Russia. This will also help ease the Russian population into Estonian society, especially those who are too old to learn. This kind of compassion will not only benefit the economy but also gain a lot of favor both domestically and abroad. A recognized language is one which is used to conduct business but not used in government proceedings. Work can help unite the country: by taking down impractical language barriers to the workplace will allow more people to work. When people work, they don't fixate on being left out of society. For example, it would be ok under this provision of hotel front desk people only spoke Russian and English for example. The current laws require hotel front desk people to speak Estonian which doesn't make such sense when tourists are coming from Russia and Europe. I have personally seen that when people from multiple backgrounds work together, they can put a face to a group and realize that everyone is pretty much the same.

Furthermore, Estonia is in a nexus between Scandinavia, Russia, Europe and even the NAFTA (North American Free Trade Area). It will benefit greatly from having a multi language capability (English and Russian primarily). As a small nation, its people can benefit from intermediating relationships between Russian enterprises and those in other nations. Finland was ruled by Sweden and they still kept Swedish as a second official language for almost 200 years without detriment to the Finnish society or culture. India was ruled by Britain and they still kept English as a recognized language.

IT outsourcing and near-sourcing is the most obvious way for Estonia to get back on the path to prosperity. Estonia has been a world leader in the IT sector, only limited by workforce capacity. Estonians are some of the most capable IT specialists; however, there just are not enough of them. The most obvious and notable accomplishment is that

Skype was written by Estonian software developers. However, now every capable IT person in the country is being fully utilized. Lack of capable work force has been the limiting factor in Estonia's quest to Europe's top five. This is the industry most stifled by the xenophobia of the current leadership. If the Estonian government allowed the immigration of IT workers from India, Philippines and perhaps even Iran, Estonia may not be in this situation. The IT sector continues to thrive and do well as demand for productivity increases. Companies turn to IT when faced with the dilemma of how to do more with less people. Instead of setting up technology embassies in Silicon Valley, the Estonian government should be setting up IT recruiting centers in developing countries and offer recruits a path to European citizenship in exchange for their skills. It will definitely yield more results on the economic bottom line.

Radio Frequency Identification (RFID) is one of the most interesting productivity boosting technologies with the potential to have many major breakthroughs that will improve our everyday life. Estonia already has extensive

GSM, Smart ID cards and wireless internet coverage which act as supporting infrastructure for RFID. The technology is an automatic identification method, relying on storing and remotely retrieving data from tags which act as transponders. The technology consists of an RFID reader and an RFID tag. An RFID tag is an object that can be applied to or incorporated into a product, animal, or person for the purpose of identification and tracking using radio waves. Some tags can be read from several meters away and beyond the line of sight of the reader. Today, RFID is used in large scale supply chain management to improve the efficiency of inventory tracking and management. Other current and widespread applications include race timing, passports and transportation payments along toll roads. Wal-Mart has mandated that all their vendors have RFID tags to streamline their logistics operations.

It has also been proposed to use RFID for point of sale store checkout to replace the cashier with an automatic system which needs no barcode scanning. This is not likely without a significant reduction in the cost of tags and changes in the POS process. There is some research taking place, however, this is some years from reaching fruition. The opportunity for Estonia is in solving the current limitations and then piloting this implementation as a showcase to companies around the world. Estonia is ideal for being a global showcase and R&D center for such technologies.

Medical Tourism, mainly Americans travelling abroad for surgery to lower their medical expenses, holds promise for the future of Estonia. Deloitte forecasts that the amount of Americans travelling overseas for medical treatment will rise from a few million patients in 2008 spending around $2B to over 17 million in 2017 spending around $50B to $80B[6]. This industry is highly fragmented with major players from ten different countries primarily India and Thailand. Lithuania for its size is already a relatively popular destination via the Baltic American Clinic. In Europe: Belgium, Poland and Slovakia are also breaking into the business with state and/or private investment. Estonia is in a position to bridge Indian doctors with American patients. Estonia would be especially attractive due to the mild summers when India is too hot and too far for people who are not well. Moreover, An Estonian clinic accredited to US standard could attract business from affluent patients within Europe and Russia. This is a complex yet feasible undertaking requiring cooperation and investment from the government, an Indian Clinic, American hospital and American health insurance companies. Recently, Air-Baltic has announced ambitions to have direct flights to the USA and the fact their existing aircraft could service the route. These think-big ideas can define the Estonian economy and act as a cash cow even during dire times.

Not only would the medical procedure be profitable but also the spillover effect resulting from tourism spending by the patients during their stay and those who accompany them. Moreover the resulting infrastructure, increased tax revenue and policies supporting this industry will raise the Estonian medical system to western standard for its entire population in terms of quality of care, pay and equipment. In conjunction to building up and gaining American standard accreditation for the clinics, an overseas American medical school similar to those in the Caribbean should be raised.

According to the Association of American Medical Colleges in 2007, of 558,053 applicants only 18,036 or around three percent matriculated into one of the approximately 130 accredited US medical schools. Many other applicants who were rejected later go to school abroad in the Caribbean, Poland and India. Most are later qualified as American Medical Association board certified doctors and pursued fruitful and rewarding careers back in the USA. The average cost and expenses associated with a public medical school range from $20,000 to well over $40,000 per year. Incidental and living expenses can almost double this cost.

There is the obvious question of certification and language. However, this is where leadership and decision making come into play. The Estonian people will have to do some "horse-trading": put the school and the clinic into English medium in exchange for access to a wider array of patients willing to pay relatively good money for their care and also contribute to the tourism business. Normally foreign medical schools are not "certified in the United States.". Instead they teach an identical curriculum and the graduates must past a foreign equivalency to practice medicine in America. The off-shore schools are rated on the percentage of their students who pass this equivalency exam. Early on, these overseas educated doctors face some obstacles compared to their American educated counterparts. However, once they prove themselves, they end up just as successful or even more so than their American educated counterparts.

The medical school will attract not only attract foreign medical students, primarily from the USA, but also top domestic students as well. Perhaps the most intelligent young Estonians will find a career in medicine more rewarding than one in usury. The domestic (Estonian) students could study for free if in exchange for practicing medicine for four years in a village or economically deprived region. The state of Kansas has such a program to bring medical care to the remote areas of the state. Estonia and especially Tallinn would be an ideal setting for an overseas medical school and clinic. If the government, local business, Indian and American entities and the local tourism sector combined efforts, they could create substantial and recession proof pillar of the Estonian economy. The combination of the clinic and medical school will lead to innovations and open many doors to prosperity. Perhaps this will lay the foundation for a biotech industry. The Mayo Clinic story is a prime example in history of how a simple ambition to provide quality medical care led to a world renowned medical institution and put the small town of Rochester, Minnesota (pop. 99, 121) on the map. I encourage readers to Google "Mayo Clinic history" as it's truly amazing story.

One of the things I enjoy most about living in Estonia is the variety and quality of candy. Estonian candy is quite unique, especially the marzipan confections. Like Switzerland, Estonia can turn candy and confections into a major export with global brand recognition. The Swiss in 2007 sold over $1.55 billion in chocolate (chocolate bars, pralines and other delightsworldwide) which is an increase 13.8% over the previous year. (Chocó Suisse - the Association of Swiss Chocolate Manufacturers).

Marzipan technology has been sitting under the noses of Estonians and under-exploited for centuries. I never seen mass produced packaged marzipan confections available in American stores. One of my personal hobbies is baking and confections. Candy may not be as sexy as hi-tech but it is a growth industry. Sales in America have been steadily growing both in aggregate and in per-capita consumption with about 35% margin according to the US Department of Commerce. The Swiss, who are the largest consumers of chocolate per capita in the world, managed to eat an average of 12.3 kilos of chocolate each, 400 grams more than the previous year according to Chocó Suisse. Warren Buffet, one of the richest men in the world, holds candy and confections companies in his portfolio: Wrigley's and See's Candies.

It would be interesting to setup an incubator concept for the candy industry. There could be a row of shops in Tallinn's old town where people from around the world can come to

Estonia, learn the basics and experiment with new ideas in the art of candy and confection making. The concept could work like this: a prospective candy entrepreneur can propose the idea he is working on. Those who are approved can use the incubators candy making facilities and secretarial services free of charge, only paying for ingredients. The incubator, owned by the Estonian government, will take share or ownership in the successful ideas. The other option is that individuals can rent or lease space in the incubator and try their ideas. This could create a whole new industry unique to Estonia: candy tourism, education and entrepreneurship.

The Nuclear Powered Future

Nuclear power will not only give Estonia energy independence but also be a cornerstone to prosperity and innovation. Cheap and reliable electricity enables industry to remain competitive. New technologies from Westinghouse and General Electric make new power plant construction as fast as three years and economically feasible. These power plants are designed with environmental safety, corporate thinking and profitability in mind. Nuclear power plants have come along way in terms of safety and performance. Chernobyl and Three Mile Island design reactors as compared to modern Westinghouse AP-1000 designs are like comparing Ford Model-T of the 1920's to modern day Hummers or Land Rovers in terms of safety and performance[7].

Nuclear power inevitably raises the questions of safety and waste management. Scientific American, a US based publication, advocates that numerous scientific studies conclude that the waste produced by coal plants is actually more radioactive than that generated by their nuclear counterparts. In fact, fly ash, a by-product from burning coal for power, contains up to 100 times more radiation than the equivalent amount nuclear waste in terms of power generated.

As for the belief that nuclear power plants emit cancer causing radiation into the environment, there exists no sufficient evidence to prove this. In fact, the amount of radiation exposure from living next to a nuclear power plant pales in comparison to the exposure we get from everyday common sources such as cosmic rays from outer space, radon gas, television sets, watch dials, smoke detectors, etc. In numbers, the average radiation dose rate people get from the before mentioned common types of radiation is ~360 millirem. The radiation dose from living next to a nuclear power plant is less than one millirem!

Uranium-235, the isotope of uranium that is used in nuclear reactors, produces 3.7 million times more energy as the equivalent amount of coal. To illustrate this point: seven trucks, each carrying six cases of two 3.7 meter high fuel assemblies, can fuel a 1000 Megawatt-electrical (MWe) reactor for 1.5 years. This plant could provide enough electricity for 1.5 million households. During this period, ~ 2 metric tons of Uranium-235 (of the 100 metric tons of fuel - uranium dioxide) would be consumed. To operate a coal plant of the same output would require one train of 89-100 ton coal cars each EVERY day. Over 350,000 tons of ash would be produced AND over 4 million tons of carbon dioxide, carbon monoxide, nitrogen oxides and sulphur oxides would be released to the environment. In summation: 3.6kg of uranium can make as much energy as 5400 Metric Tons (MT) of oil or 7800 MT of Coal.

Around 96% of the spent nuclear fuel can be effectively recycled. A typical large (1000 MWe) light water reactor will produce about $20m^3$ (27 tonnes) of used fuel per year, which corresponds to a $75m^3$ disposal volume following encapsulation if it is treated as waste. Where if that same volume spent fuel is reprocessed, only $3m^3$ of vitrified waste (glass) is produced, which is equivalent to a $28m^3$ disposal volume following placement in a disposal canister.

Nuclear and coal energy are the only economically viable large scale solutions to growing energy demand. Wind, solar, geothermal, hydro all have limitations by geography, price and scale. The choice is clear, do we keep pumping large heaps of soot and ash into the atmosphere where it reaps havoc in the atmosphere or do we opt to consolidate and isolate nuclear waste deep underground,. It will be kept away from any present and future society in a controlled manner which can be monitored. The nuclear power industry, politicians and academia must make the public aware of this choice in a very crystal clear manner.

Thorium reactor technology advances are making this technology more viable. Thorium which is four times as abundant as Uranium, more proliferation resistant while costing less than current technologies was limited by the fact there was no efficient or economical way to keep the neutron counts high enough to sustain the chain reaction essential to nuclear fission. Thorium Power, a Washington DC based firm, mixed Thorium with Uranium and other fissile materials to get around this issue. Nobel Prize winner Carlos Rubbia proposed to use a particle accelerator to kick start the reaction. This technology is holds promise to lower waste levels and reduce costs.

A nuclear plant could not only could deliver all the electricity needs for Estonia, the excess capacity could be sold to neighboring countries and/or used to create hydrogen fuel via electrolysis (the process to separate water into its hydrogen and oxygen components). This plant would require massive investments from the government, private sector and the European Union. It will be one of the most essential measures to realizing the dream to be among the five richest nations in Europe. The electrical grid will need to be updated and initially engineers and technicians will need to be recruited from abroad. Eventually the profits gained from this initiative could be reinvested into the education system to grow this talent domestically.

This potential new found ability for Estonia to create hydrogen fuel with zero CO_2 emissions in a relatively cheap manner could lay the groundwork for Estonia to be one of the first nations to enter into the hydrogen economy. Just as Estonia was a proving ground for IT and telecom technologies, it could also be a proving ground for the hydrogen powered cars, busses and the associated infrastructure such as the filling stations. Subsequently, this would attract large auto players like Tata, Ford, BMW, Toyota, Mercedes Benz, etc who would in turn create many high value R&D, engineering and technical jobs. This participation in the inevitable hydrogen revolution could propel Estonia to a position of scientific leadership.

National Defense and Individual Initiative

Peace and security for all the Baltic nations will come at the end of a gun. Estonians will need to change their paradigms when it comes to national defense and sovereignty. Great nations evoke great amounts of envy and inevitably become intertwined on the global stage. I would suggest adapting a second amendment to create a well armed society where the common citizens have the ability to take it upon themselves to pose a challenge to any invader or domestic government that wants to bring back the USSR.

The second amendment (The right to bear arms) of the US Constitution was created for that very reason; give the citizens a means to overthrow a government that becomes tyrannical and which no longer serves the best interests of its citizenry. This is part of the fabric of the US Constitutional system of checks and balances which keeps the government accountable to its citizens. My observations of European attitude are that they are more willing to give concessions to an invader rather than stand up. The current rift in Europe on how to deal with Russia is evidence enough that Estonia, perhaps in alliance with the other Baltic nations, should take care of their own defense initiatives.

Freedom is not free. Estonian men need to understand that military service to their country is the price that must be paid for the right to vote, speak freely and pursue happiness. National defense will need to be priority of each Estonian and participation in the military will be needed by all males at the very least to ensure the existence of the nation for future generations.

The current state of affairs with the Russian military can be exploited. The Russian army is mostly broken down and made up of mostly disenchanted individuals. The state of the Russian military is one mired in disarray and corruption. The US State Department contends that the Russian military salaries are low, ranging from $250-$350/month for regular soldiers and up to $560/month for professionals. Theoretically, the army provides all necessities, but housing and food shortages continue to plague the armed forces. Problems with both discipline and brutal hazing are common as well. Such conditions continue to encourage draft evasion and efforts to delay military service. Moreover, military officials complain that new recruit cohorts are plagued by increasing incidences of poor education, communicable diseases, and criminality. HIV infection rates in the Russian army are estimated to be between two and five times higher than in the general population and tuberculosis is a persistent problem. The Russian Government has stated a desire to convert to a professional army, but implementation has been progressing slowly. There is also an effort to develop a non-commissioned officer (NCO) corps, but the military faces difficulties recruiting NCOs, and has done little to develop the mechanisms and capability to sustain such a force.

With proper publicity (psychological warfare), individual soldiers who are already not feeling too happy about their lives will desert when faced with the reality that every Estonian man and perhaps every woman pose a major risk to their lives. This would lead to breakdowns in enemy command and control which would further favor the defender (Estonia).

Moreover, nations that stand up and fight are far more respected than those that route. Furthermore if Estonians put up a fight, it would inspire men from all parts of Europe, America and other parts of the free world to come the aid of the Estonians. There is a Biblical saying that God helps those who help themselves. If Estonian individuals and the collective voice of the government make it clear that they will not back down if invaded, they can perhaps even build constructive a relationship with Russia based on mutual respect.

Switzerland which has been around since 1291 is an amazing country in which Estonia could also look to for guidance on nation building. It is ranked second on The Global Competitiveness Index the (World Economic Forum) just after the United States. It is nation with very few natural resources but it has one of the highest per-capita GDP's in the world. Switzerland is well known for pharmaceuticals, precision manufacturing, tourism, banking, food and confections. There are four official languages: German, Italian, French and Romansh. English is considered by many as the fifth unofficial language. Tourists and foreign businessmen may express themselves in English and stand a good chance to get answered. In some multinational companies located in Switzerland, English has been declared as corporate language, especially if their customers speak English anyway. Sometimes even native Swiss people with different mother tongues (German vs. French or Italian) will use some English words as a common basis.

Direct democracy is one of the most unique characteristics to Switzerland and it should be considered in Estonia. The system is defined in the 1848 federal constitution. Swiss citizens are subject to three legal jurisdictions: the commune, canton and federal levels. The instruments of Swiss direct democracy at the federal level, known as civil rights, include the right to submit a constitutional initiative and a referendum, both of which may overturn parliamentary decisions.

By calling a federal referendum a group of citizens may challenge a law that has been passed by Parliament, if they can collect 50,000 signatures against the law within 100 days. If so, a national vote is scheduled where voters decide by a simple majority whether to accept or reject the law. Eight cantons together can also call a referendum on a federal law.

Similarly, the federal constitutional initiative allows citizens to put a constitutional amendment to a national vote, if they can get 100,000 voters to sign the proposed amendment within 18 months. Parliament can supplement the proposed amendment with a counter-proposal, with voters having to indicate a preference on the ballot in case both proposals are accepted. Constitutional amendments, whether introduced by initiative or in Parliament, must be accepted by a double majority of both the national popular vote and a majority of the cantonal popular votes

The Swiss have peacefully maintained a culture of independence since 1674. However, the peace gained from un-involvement in neighboring conflicts required rigorous investment in national defense. Switzerland's national defense is an excellent example of how a small nation, with significant participation from its citizens, can protect itself without relying empty promises from an ad-hoc alliance. The military officers in full-time service make up intervention companies, which can be mobilized quickly to be engaged in operations. The militiamen are divided up in reserve formations that represent nearly a quarter of a brigade's battalions. They are subjected to obligatory annual rifle training and keep their assault rifle and their munitions (only accessible in time of war) in their homes. Only the command-structure of the formations of reserve is active. In the event of a major crisis, the Federal Counsel and Parliament make the decision on whether or not to activate the reserve units.

Patrick Henry was a prominent figure in the American Revolution, known and remembered for his "Give me Liberty, or give me Death!" speech. It's about backing your ideals with your blood; this is the essence in building national pride for future generations. The Georgians have demonstrated that there is a lack of ability in many of the new Central and Eastern European democracies to back up their words and rhetoric with actions. In the recent conflict, the five million Georgian citizens outnumbered the 20,000 Russian invaders at a ratio 250 to 1. They managed cede a substantial amount of real estate in less than a week. Historically, successful invasion forces need three times the amount of defenders to win. Ho Chi Min (Vietnam) and the Afghan mujahedeen demonstrated quite well that even superpowers can be defeated by the smallest of nations.

If all Estonians demonstrated a willingness to viciously and violently stand up to an invading force even when faced with loss, it will send a clear message that aggression and the following occupation will be costly. War is about the balance between blood and treasure. Nations at war are calculating the cost in lives (it takes 20 years to make a soldier) and the economic cost. History has shown that nations can win every battle but end up losing the war: i.e. the Vietnam War. In other words, victory can be made so costly for an invader that an attacking army can win every battle but go bankrupt in the process, leading to the victorious nation's demise.

In the ancient Greek battle of Thermopylae fought in 480BC, three hundred Spartans held off more than a million Persian invaders for almost three days. Although the 300 Spartans defenders were annihilated, news of Spartans heroic defense, which took 20,000 Persian lives, sent shockwaves and disrupted morale throughout the Persian army and eventually led to the decline of the Persian Empire. It will take time and a strong leader to build up such a system but it is highly feasible if everyone believes in the cause.

Russians respects strength as evidenced by the by the Finnish Winter War in 1939. On November 30, 1939 250,000 Russian troops under the cover of a coordinated air and artillery bombardment crossed into Finland to begin one of the most costly campaigns in military history. It would be a "walk over;" General Meretskov estimated it would take only 10 to 12 days for his 26 well equipped 14,000 man divisions to reach Helsinki. Opposing him were nine poorly equipped 11,000-man Finnish divisions.

Meretskov never suspected that his army was about to plunge into a frozen hell, the second coldest winter since 1828, and oppose Mannerheim, probably one of the greatest defensive tacticians since Robert E. Lee. For 105 days the world held its breath while Russian soldiers died at the incredible rate of nearly 10,000 per day and the Finns lost 250 per day. When the armistice finally came on March 13, 1940, the Finns counted 25,000 dead, 55,000 wounded and 450,000 homeless, a terrible price for a country of only four million people. All this was at the hands of an army of less than 250,000 (mostly light infantry and local militia units) with hardly any anti-tank weapons except Molotov cocktails and 41 operational fighter aircraft. The Russians never tried to intimidate Finland after this.

Russia is economically about six times smaller than the EU. (EU GDP is around $12T with a population of 500M and Russian GDP is around $2T with a population of 140M). It is laughable how much pressure they exert on the EU. By carrying a "big stick and speaking softly" (Teddy Roosevelt), Estonia should inspire other European nations and the individual men within to adapt the same stance of striving for peace while having the willingness and readiness to fight if attacked.

Strategically, the root of the national defense problem is with Europe's energy dependence. Russia uses energy to play the Germans among others against the EU members. This problem can be addressed by a nuclear power. The "Power Paradox" states that power is defined by how much one nation gives the other. It further states that every time power is used, some of it is lost. As Russia exploits Europe's fractured Union, the Europeans should find solutions for the future – better known as a work around.

Operationally, the Estonian government needs to invest into Stinger and Patriot air defense systems and the Predator and Reaper unmanned aerial vehicles (UAV). Armed UAVs are not only a very lethal weapon but it also a physcological weapon. An invader will be less willing to fight a merciless robot, and the morale of the Estonian army will be boosted by the fact they can see over the horizon.

Tactically, Estonia should take its own initiative to work with Blackwater International and Israeli Defense Forces (IDF) to master the use of such weapons and tactics. But first, the spiritual problem must be solved. Estonian and European men in general need to step-up to military service if they want to keep this society intact and free from aggression and manipulation. his military doctrine combined with an inclusive and tolerant society will sway the loyalty of indigenous Russians to Estonia.

"I may disagree with what you have to say, but I shall defend to the death your right to say it" (Voltaire) Most everyone wants to belong to a winning team, that not only tolerates dissenting pointing of view but also uses them to change and strengthen the society. It's not about what the person is saying but the fact that people can speak openly about matters close to their heart that must be defended.

Currently, most Russians in Estonia understand their life in Estonia is better than life in Russia. Baltic Russians are treated like second class citizens in Russia, especially in Moscow due to their accent. Estonia can use this to their favor in building loyalty to the Estonian homeland. Most

Russian I have encountered feel backed into a corner by the current government policy, media attacks and sentiment despite the fact most ethnic Russians are working, paying taxes and living peacefully. Thus they feel frustration from both sides and fall back on nostalgic feelings of Soviet and Russian propaganda to lash out against Estonia. Furthermore, by gaining the loyalty of its own Russian population, Estonia can further deter the current Russian administration from trying any theatrics.

Eventually, the ethnic Russian, foreigners and native Estonians will form cohesive bonds during military service that will promote tolerance and understanding and lead to life long friendships. All of us who have done military service understand that the stress of training, exercises and battle binds people from diverse backgrounds together for life. We focus under stress on what we have in common rather than what makes us different and work together to press forward and win. Military service not only provides a means of defense for a nation but it also helps educate leaders. Estonia should consider using the military as a leadership development program to increase the pool of capable domestic decision makers.

The ROTC (Reserve Officer Training Corps.) system is a college-based, officer commissioning program used mostly in the US. It is designed as a college elective that focuses on leadership development, problem solving, strategic planning, and professional ethics. The GI Bill is a similar program where the member joins the military for four years and in exchange is given a university education and support in exchange. Furthermore, the GI Bill allows all those who done service to take a home loan with 0% down and gives them preferential hiring in public sector jobs. These programs have allowed many people to better their own lives and society at the same time. Such education for service programs could be implemented in Estonia in the form of Western education in exchange for four years of military service. This will fill the long term needs for leadership in politics, government and the military itself.

There are two aspects to success: attitudes and skills. One can learn skills but attitude must come from within. Successful business leaders all over the world will tell you that it's easier to work with a person who is enthusiastic and honest but lacks skills than a clever person who cannot be trusted. Trust is the basis to delegation of authority which enables companies to grow on layered management. A person who can admit he doesn't know and is able to influence a specialist will be far more valuable than a person with a high IQ who can't communicate when there is a problem. Over time, skills are learned and experience is gained. However, if a person lacks character, they will just create more elaborate or convoluted schemes over time.

The military concentrates its training into developing the 14 basic leadership attributes: justice, judgment, dependability, initiative, decisiveness tact, integrity, enthusiasm, bearing, unselfishness, courage, knowledge, loyalty and endurance. Leaders with these attributes ingrained into their character will do more to build a nation than high powered lawyers or MBA's.

The departing military leaders, who fulfilled their minimum obligation, can fill the leadership needs in corporate Estonia or the government. Korn/Ferry International (a US based consulting firm) and the Economist Intelligence Unit conducted a study to identify the major traits that characterize ex-military CEOs and suggest that deft management of stressful situations in the real-world setting of military operations may well enhance performance in a corporate environment. They found that military officers are over-represented among the ranks of CEOs. Chief executives who served as military officers constitute 8.4% of the S&P 500 in 2005, compared to only 3% of all US adult males who served as officers.

Religion & Economics

Economics, in my view, is the study and quantification of the collision between human physcology and mathematics. One Cambridge University professor summed up the fact that economics is driven on two very basic human emotions: fear and greed. I interpreted this to be lack of faith and arrogance. Faith allows people to moderate the two emotional economic drivers by allowing people to be thankful when times are good and draw on belief and family for courage when times are bad, allowing them to rationally stay on course or even embark on new ventures.

I am a strong believer of the First Amendment (the separation of church and state) of the US Constitution. This has allowed religion to flourish in the United States by the fact that people are stronger in their beliefs when they choose it for themselves versus having it imposed. It is imperative that governments allow people to believe and worship what they want. European nations must tolerate as equals Evangelical Christians, Hasidic Jews, Hare Krishna's, Muslims, Jehovah's Witnesses, Mormons, and all others if they want to be true democracies. The limiting of religious or ideological expression just retrenches Europe's chronic cultural integration problems.

Democracy is not about giving things away or guaranteed entitlements. It is about letting people find their own way, express themselves freely without fear of reprisal, creating fairness and a level playing field for all. The rest is up to the individual in terms of how far they want to go.

Religion has been used as justification to conduct many of the world's atrocities and injustices. However, Europeans, on an individual level, should reconsider downplaying the importance of religion. After all, it was faith that gave the Polish people and Lek Walensa inner strength to push the "Solidarity" demonstrations in the shipyards of Gdansk. Through Pope John Paul II's unwavering words of compassion and forgiveness which he spoke while having rifles pointed directly at him; the Soviet Union started to crumble. It was also faith that drove the Afghan Mujahedeen and enlisted support from the Islamic and free world to oust the Soviet Union. If a country has the wrong ideology, no matter how much firepower it has, it is doomed to crumble from within.

The strength of a nation comes from the collective support of the people who make up the society. If the national ideology is in-line with the citizens beliefs', the society can only succeed. It becomes an extension of the persons being and worthy of support and defense. However, if the national ideology hammers its citizens, it won't take much to bring it down.

Many European countries, including Estonia offer "mother salaries" or have laws where men and women can take over a years worth of leave to be with their newborn kids. Many Scandinavian countries even offer free, state supported day care. The American government and system in general offers very limited support to mothers, mostly those with very low income, blindness or some other ailment. The terms of leave mostly depend on the persons employer. Despite the superior European family support, the United States fertility rate recently hit a 35 year high and remains substantially higher than European birth rates according to

US Government and UN statistics (Birthrate in the USA is ~2.10 and in the EU is ~1.5). Experts believe that most of this can be attributed to the stronger religious values and the perception that family is not career hindrance. "Americans are much more religious than Europeans: They believe in God more. They go to church more," said Charles Westoff, a Princeton University demographer. "That sort of religious attitude or set of values is strongly correlated with fertility." In my own experience from living in Europe, it amazes me how many Europeans hold the view that believing in God is for uneducated or illiterate people. I advise a close reexamination of this subject as these critics seem to be missing the most important point of our existence. "Those who stand for nothing fall for anything" (Alexander Hamilton).

Trust is the most important aspect of society and it's the basis to empowerment and love. Trust starts at home and then its permutated throughout the society. With trust people can work without supervision, work gets done and companies and societies prosper. My personal observations are that people drink much less and have more focus when they have confidence in their relationships and families. People have a sense of direction and purpose which gives them happiness. Thus a society should focus on making the family strong and guarding trust. If you fix the home then you fix the nation.

Tax breaks and incentive should be targeted to encourage the building of family units. Families tend to be a source of strength and a sense of security which can enable a nation to move forward. Moreover, the paternity rules should be strengthened so that men who choose not to be responsible fathers still have to contribute the child's well being financially. Modern DNA testing and the state of the art banking system should make it easy to identify dead-beat fathers and garnish their wages.

Infidelity and alcoholism are other issues that affect the economy at its core. Infidelity creates suspicion and distrust in the home which is then permutated throughout the society. In many cases, it leads to heavy drinking to dampen the emotional pain and resulting depression. The perpetrator has to cover up his misdeeds and in many cases family resources are diverted outside the home to the mistress. He may have to drink heavily to cover up his dilemmas about the vow's he took versus his short term physical or egotistical needs. The collective effects of "micro-corruption" lead to instability, depression and drunkenness which strain the family and leads to a loss of sleep and the ability to concentrate. Certainly if there are kids involved, it could make them synclinal and apathetic towards life, relationships and work further tainting the society. There is no direct connection to my assertion; the evidence is highly circumstantial. If one thinks about it logically on a personal level then multiplies the aggregate effects thereof across a nation, this could lend an explanation to why there is a lot of alcoholism, depression, abnormally high suicide rates, relatively high HIV rate, mistrust, corruption and relatively low productivity in the workplace in Estonia.

According to an Estonian Institute of Economic Research survey a few years ago, the statistics show that in 12 years, Estonia has lost 45,700 people between the ages of 15 and 49 years due to alcoholism. A recent study undertaken by the Geneva Declaration shows that the murder rate in Estonia (6.82 per 100,000 inhabitants per year in 2004) is higher than the United States (5.7 per 100,000 per year inhabitants in 2006), the nation with the highest rate of gun ownership and Finland (2.75 per 100,000 inhabitants per year in 2004). The most disturbing statistic is the high rate of suicides in all three Baltic nations. According to the World Health Organization in 2005, the Baltics had some of the highest suicide rates in the world: Lithuania topped the list with 38.6 suicides per 100,000 people per year, Latvia had 24.5 per 100,000 people per year and Estonia had 20.3 per 100,000 people per year. The suicide rate in the United States is 11.0 per 100,000 people per year. This is something that no country can afford, but is especially true for the thinly populated Baltic nations.

I always believed religion is the magic of American society that enables it to overcome and surprise so many in the darkest of hours, especially when faced with so many obstacles such as lower literacy rates, poverty, internal strife, etc. Most American Presidents including Barack Obama, Nobel Prize winning scientists, CEO's, self-made billionaires acknowledge that they believe in God and heaven and hell whether it is Christian, Jewish, Muslim, Hindu or another faith. Faith gives us the strength and courage to reach out to new comers and people in need on an individual basis. This may explain why immigrants are happier and feel more accepted in the US vs. Europe despite the lack of financial support.

Faith when chosen of free will and applied in the right and humble way empowers individuals and allows us to draw strength and to turn chaos into order.

The Role of Americans in Estonia

Ironically, much of Estonia's predicament is due to American policy. The Americans managed to send their consumerism but not their winning ideology. Somewhere we failed to reveal what it really takes to achieve this dream of prosperity. Our government never advocated that the citizenship policy for indigenous Russians clearly contradicts the American way. How can people (native Russians and some others) who are born, hold a job and pay taxes to Estonia (these taxes are used to build monuments) be denied citizenship and the right to vote? We criticize and sanction China, Bangladesh and other nations for violating human rights but we don't seem to apply this policy to many of the new European nations?

Every American should be troubled by this fact of how a country can deny citizenship by birth to a certain ethnic group of people. We had this track record before with our long tolerance of the apartheid in South Africa. It took the American government and unusually long time to pressure South Africa into allowing free elections for all. Whatever the reasons, the ethnic Russians that were born in Estonia are entitled to a national birthright. We should have taught that people on an individual basis that reaching out with a hand of friendship to their Russian neighbors could change the tone dramatically. Peace and reconciliation will not come from the government but from the collective change in heart of each individual.

The stateless people should be offered political asylum in the United States. The Soviet Union was not their fault. In fact, Russians were the largest ethnic component in the Siberian gulags. If Estonians are so worried about losing their culture, this policy of two citizen classes will be sure to destroy it from within. It is time to start integrating all schools and work at a high level to create programs for mutual understanding. TV shows, team sports for young people and youth exchanges can help break down these barriers. Not only have I personally witnessed Israelis and Palestinians come together in the USA but also Estonians with Russian ethnicity and Estonians. People can get along; it's just a matter of will and creating the right environment.

American government officials when meeting with Estonian government leaders should point out areas for improvement instead of encouraging provocation with Russia and offering hollow promises of NATO defense. Everyone, except the Baltic government officials and people, understands that NATO Article 5 is a joke. The article is loosely worded language that each member can respond as they deem adequate. In reality, the Baltics should rename the alliance as YOYO: You're On Your Own.

American officials need to show Estonian leaders a more efficient way to prosperity by drawing on examples of our successes in peace and mediation such as the Camp David Peace Accord which was facilitated by Jimmy Carter and signed by Egypt and Israel and from our mistakes such as our failed ventures into Iraq and Vietnam. We as Americans not only allowed but almost encouraged this dangerous game of chicken with Russia. Estonians should be aware that, like the EU, the Americans are considering Estonia only as piece of a larger strategy. The Americans are not considering Estonia's best interests. Most

Americans don't even know where Estonia is let alone care about it. There are plenty of examples in history when the Americans went back on their promises: Bay of Pigs in Cuba and the Kurdish Uprising in Iraq and many more.

Estonia can achieve greatness much more efficiently if it incorporates the best practices learns from the mistakes from other nations. The lack of both political and business leadership to understand simple diplomacy, human rights and long term strategic planning is surprising considering the amount of American educators, military advisors and investors present in Estonia. I remember talking over lunch to an American professor who teaches business at one of the local universities in Tallinn and a former head of the American Chamber of Commerce about the subject of not only teaching basic business principals but also the cultural values that made America the most innovative and prosperous nation in the history of the planet. They laughed and said that if Estonia ever got rich it would be harder to get the pretty girls. They may have been joking but this highlights the fact that even the American foreigners here have their own agenda.

These are the core philosophies that enabled America to rise from colony to superpower: the belief that nationality is an ideology not genetic; that all people are equal under the law and God; flexibility and self-criticism are necessary for advancement; look to the future for your dreams instead of dwelling on the nightmares of the past and mostly that anything is possible if you work at it. There are many more beliefs but the most American value we can impart is that only Estonians can help Estonia at the end of the day.

What is Culture Anyway?

Home is not a geographic concept, but something we all carry inside ourselves (A.D. Sinjawsky). Culture by dictionary definition is the integrated pattern of human knowledge, belief, and behaviour that depends upon the capacity for learning and transmitting knowledge to succeeding generations. It can be transmitted to anyone. The problem in Estonia is this last part about succeeding generations. Current depopulation trends could destabilize the country leading to a chain of events that make it economically unviable for investors and cause a mass exodus, thus putting the long term preservation of this culture at risk. Change and adaptation is hard to accept and even harder to execute but it must be done to ensure survival of Estonian culture. If one looks back on history, the greatest societies and organizations in existence today have underwent not only one but many periods of change and adjustment.

Get over it and get one with life. Estonians can keep on ignoring the world around them and remain relatively

110

isolated, bitter and inflexible. They can keep on feeling sorry for themselves about the Soviet times. But bear in mind, there is no law or rule that anyone or any nation owes Estonia anything for its tormented past. In fact, all the help and aid from the West is voluntary and almost a favor on their part. Moreover, suffering and persecution is a fact of life for many around the world: past, present and even in the future. For example, in recent time there was great suffering on the same or greater magnitude than the Soviet occupation among the Kosovo Albanians, Rwandans, Iraqi's, North Koreans to name a few. There are great lessons of history freely available which can save hundreds of years of guesswork and let people get on with life and their pursuit of prosperity. Or Estonians can, by inaction, choose continued suffering and go unnoticed through the annals of history. People and nations everywhere have problems of their own; hence they can only offer limited help.

No one can force change. "You can do whatever you want", but don't be disappointed by the resulting consequences: little or no real growth, low social mobility and reduced optimism. This will reduce Estonia's significance and lead to its abandonment from the outside world, thus putting the nation and culture at greater risk. Ironically, the current Estonian culture is killing Estonia. Instead the nation and its people can choose once again to be a revolutionary model for the rest of Europe, resulting in a revived dynamic economy where people are judged on merit and a society where all those who are willing to work and contribute are welcomed and included into the social and cultural fabric. But this will also offer its own set of challenges. Life for individuals, families, businesses and nations is about choices, considerations and decisions.

What is ironic is that Estonian culture thrived in Toronto during the occupation. The Estonian parliament, although in exile, went about its business, the language was being taught and the culture was institutionalized. Similarly, Lithuanian culture did the same in Chicago. Culture is not only transferable among people but also among locations. The fact that Estonian culture survived the trauma of the Soviet occupation is a strong enough argument it will survive immigration and the building of a multicultural society. We must remember that all children are born innocent and without any grudge. It's important to teach them to look forward with optimism and help them understand history is for learning lessons, not grounding hate and animosity.

At first Estonia will have to import world class leadership talent but then it can eventually be created at home. This will give rise to a proverbial "Estonian Harvard" where world class scientists, leaders, doctors, engineers, scientists and philosophers are educated not only for Estonia but for the world. Estonia then will be a source and destination for top talent. Nothing could ensure the continuity of Estonian culture for generations more than institutionalizing it into the fabric of global society. Estonians should not be afraid to think big.

Mystery, a world famous celebrity pick up artist, tells his students on a VH1 reality show, "if you keep doing what you're doing, you're going to keep getting what you get." I wrote this piece not only because I really care about Estonia but also to encourage its people to think different. I hope that Estonians can free themselves from the bondages of resentment, bitterness and xenophobia. If a nation is ever to emerge to western standard, the mentality of its people must rise to western standard as well. Everything I wrote is doable and just a matter of will. It all starts with getting the facts and taking an active role in the society. Estonia holds great promise and I believe it could be richer than Luxembourg if the right series of decisions are made.

– Alexander Grover

Appendix 1: US States as Nations

US State or EU Nation	2007 GDP-PPP (billions USD)	2006 Population	GDP-PPP per Capita (USD)	2007 GDP Growth	Fertility Rate (Most Recent)
US - District of Columbia	93.82	588,282	$159,480	4.3	<1.9
EU - Luxembourg	38.14	480,222	$79,422	4.6	1.78
US - Delaware	60.12	864,764	$69,520	-1.6	2.00
US - Alaska	44.52	683,478	$65,133	0.3	>2.2
US - Connecticut	216.27	3,502,309	$61,750	2.8	1.90
US - Wyoming	31.51	522,830	$60,276	1.8	2.10
US - New York	1,103.02	19,297,729	$57,158	4.4	1.90
EU*- Norway	246.6	4,644,457	$55,600	4.9	1.90
US - Massachusetts	351.51	6,449,755	$54,500	2.5	<1.9
US - New Jersey	465.48	8,685,920	$53,591	1.1	2.10
US - Louisiana	216.15	4,293,204	$50,346	2.6	2.00
US - Virginia	382.96	7,712,091	$49,658	1.9	2.00
US - California	1,812.97	36,553,215	$49,598	1.5	2.10
US - Nevada	127.21	2,565,382	$49,588	0.6	>2.2
US - Minnesota	254.97	5,197,621	$49,055	2.2	2.00
US - Colorado	236.32	4,861,515	$48,611	2.0	2.10
US - Washington	311.27	6,468,424	$48,121	4.3	1.90
US - Hawaii	61.53	1,283,388	$47,945	3.0	>2.2
US - Maryland	268.69	5,618,344	$47,823	2.0	2.00
US - Texas	1,141.97	23,904,380	$47,772	4.1	>2.2
US - Illinois	609.57	12,852,548	$47,428	1.5	2.10
EU - Ireland	191.60	4,109,086	$46,628	5.0	1.85
United States - All	13,860.00	301,139,947	$46,025	2.0	2.09
US - Nebraska	80.09	1,774,571	$45,134	2.1	>2.2
US - Rhode Island	46.90	1,057,832	$44,336	-0.1	<1.9
US - North Carolina	399.45	9,061,032	$44,084	2.2	2.00
US - New Hampshire	57.34	1,315,828	$43,578	-0.1	<1.9
US - North Dakota	27.73	639,715	$43,340	3.0	1.90

US State or EU Nation	2007 GDP-PPP (billions USD)	2006 Population	GDP-PPP per Capita (USD)	2007 GDP Growth	Fertility Rate (Most Recent)
US - Pennsylvania	531.11	12,432,792	$42,718	1.6	1.90
US - South Dakota	33.93	796,214	$42,619	2.3	>2.2
US - Kansas	117.31	2,775,997	$42,257	2.8	>2.2
US - Oregon	158.23	3,747,455	$42,224	3.2	1.90
US - Georgia	396.50	9,544,750	$41,542	2.8	2.10
US - Wisconsin	232.29	5,601,640	$41,469	1.0	1.90
US - Ohio	466.31	11,466,917	$40,666	0.4	2.00
US - Florida	734.52	18,251,243	$40,245	0.0	2.00
US - Utah	105.57	2,645,330	$39,907	5.3	>2.2
EU* - Switzerland	303.2	7,581,520	$39,800	2.6	1.44
US - Tennessee	243.87	6,156,719	$39,610	0.9	2.00
US - Vermont	24.54	621,254	$39,506	1.5	<1.9
EU - Austria	322.00	8,199,783	$39,269	2.8	1.38
US - Missouri	229.47	5,878,415	$39,036	1.3	2.10
US - Arizona	247.03	6,338,755	$38,971	1.8	>2.2
EU - Netherlands	645.50	16,570,613	$38,955	4.7	1.98
US - Indiana	246.44	6,345,289	$38,838	0.3	2.10
US - New Mexico	76.18	1,969,915	$38,671	2.8	>2.2
US - Oklahoma	139.32	3,617,316	$38,516	4.0	2.10
Canada	1,326.38	33,390,141	$38,200	2.7	1.57
US - Michigan	381.96	10,071,822	$37,924	-1.2	1.90
EU - Sweden	338.50	9,031,088	$37,482	2.7	1.67
EU - Denmark	203.30	5,468,120	$37,179	1.9	1.80
US - Maine	48.11	1,317,207	$36,523	1.3	<1.9
US - Kentucky	154.18	4,241,474	$36,352	2.3	2.00
EU - Belgium	376.50	10,392,226	$36,229	2.7	1.65
EU - Finland	188.40	5,238,460	$35,965	1.5	1.83
US - Alabama	165.80	4,627,851	$35,826	1.8	1.90
US - Montana	34.25	957,861	$35,760	3.5	2.00
EU - United Kingdom	2,130.00	60,776,238	$35,047	2.9	1.91
US - South Carolina	152.83	4,407,709	$34,673	2.0	1.90
US - Idaho	51.15	1,499,402	$34,113	2.4	>2.2

116

US State or EU Nation	2007 GDP-PPP (billions USD)	2006 Population	GDP-PPP per Capita (USD)	2007 GDP Growth	Fertility Rate (Most Recent)
Japan	4,376.71	127,433,494	$33,800	2.0	1.22
EU - Spain	1,361.00	40,448,191	$33,648	3.8	1.41
EU - France	2,075.00	63,718,187	$32,565	2.0	1.89
US - West Virginia	57.71	1,812,035	$31,849	0.1	<1.9
EU - Italy	1,800.00	58,147,733	$30,956	1.8	1.38
EU - Greece	327.60	10,706,290	$30,599	3.8	1.33
US - Mississippi	88.55	2,918,785	$30,337	1.7	2.00
European Union - All	14,430.00	490,426,060	$29,423	2.8	1.50
EU - Slovenia	56.19	2,009,245	$27,966	4.5	1.28
EU - Cyprus	21.40	788,457	$27,142	3.9	1.61
US - Arkansas	95.37	3,834,797	$24,870	1.5	2.10
EU - Czech Republic	251.00	10,228,744	$24,539	4.8	1.23
S. Korea	1,196.00	48,850,000	$24,500	5.0	1.20
EU - Malta	9.40	401,880	$23,390	2.3	1.51
EU - Portugal	232.30	10,642,836	$21,827	1.8	1.49
EU - Estonia	28.69	1,315,912	$21,802	9.9	1.42
EU - Slovakia	110.20	5,447,502	$20,229	8.2	1.34
EU - Hungary	191.70	9,956,108	$19,255	2.8	1.34
EU - Latvia	40.05	2,259,810	$17,723	10.5	1.29
EU - Lithuania	59.98	3,575,439	$16,776	7.0	1.22
EU - Poland	623.10	38,518,241	$16,177	6.5	1.27
FSU-Russia	2097	140,702,096	$14,800	8.1	1.40
Iran	270.94	65,397,521	$12,300	5.4	1.71
EU - Bulgaria	86.71	7,322,858	$11,841	6.0	1.40
EU - Romania	247.10	22,276,056	$11,093	6.5	1.38
FSU-Belarus	103.5	9,685,768	$10,600	8.2	1.25
Brazil	1,314.17	196,342,592	$9,700	5.7	2.22
Turkey	612.30	71,158,647	$9,400	4.5	1.89
FSU-Ukraine	324.8	45,994,288	$7,000	7.7	1.25
China	3,280.05	1,321,851,888	$5,300	11.9	1.77
India	1,170.97	1,129,866,154	$3,800	9.0	2.76

Source: IMF, World Bank, CIA Factbook, UN, US Census Bureau

Footnotes & References

Footnotes:

1. Ian Traynor, (September 18, 2008*). The Guardian Anti-Semitism and Islamophobia rising across Europe, survey finds.*
   http://www.guardian.co.uk/world/2008/sep/18/islam.religion

2. Ironman (2008), *2007 US vs. EU GDP-PPP Cage Match Contest*
   http://politicalcalculations.blogspot.com/search?q=2007+GDP

3. US Patent and Trademark Office (2007), *Patents By Country, State, and Year - All Patent Types*
   http://www.uspto.gov/go/taf/cst_all.htm

4. Wikipedia (2008), *List of countries and territories by fertility rate*
   http://en.wikipedia.org/wiki/List_of_countries_and_territories_by_fertility_rate

5. Wikipedia (2008), *Evil Empire*
   http://en.wikipedia.org/wiki/Evil_empire

6. Paul H. Keckley, PhD, Deloitte (2007) *Medical Tourism – Consumers in Search of Value.*
   http://www.deloitte.com/dtt/cda/doc/content/sr_Medical_tourism%281%29.pdf

7. Westinghouse Nuclear (2008), *AP-1000*
    http://www.ap1000.westinghousenuclear.com/

References:

Population, Politics Industry and Innovation:

The United States Constitution
http://www.archives.gov/exhibits/charters/constitution.html

Alan F. Kay, PhD, The Polling Critic (June 27, 2005), *EU Constitution, a Tragic Voting Process ~ #53*
http://www.cdi.org/polling/53-EU-Constitution.cfm

Andrew Rettman: EU Observer (May 2, 2007) *Estonia calls for EU help on Russia embassy siege*
http://euobserver.com/9/23972

Eduard Vaht, (November 22, 2007) *Open Letter to Ansip*
http://peaminister.blogspot.com/

Joel Alas, The Baltic Times (September 19, 2007), *Tartu faces number crunch*
http://www.baltictimes.com/news/articles/18828

Joel Alas, The Baltic Times (October 31, 2007) *Ansip dogged by communist past*
http://www.baltictimes.com/news/articles/19166 /

Wikipedia (2008) Arnold Rüütel
http://en.wikipedia.org/wiki/Arnold_R%C3%BC%C3%BCtel

George Koo, New American Media (January 25, 2006),
*Silicon Valley's Lead Role in Idea Economy Relies on
Foreign-Born*
http://www.imdiversity.com/villages/Careers/employment_
trends/pns_immigration_silicon_valley_0106.asp

Johan Norberg, The National Interest, online edition (June 1,
2006) *Swedish Models*
http://www.nationalinterest.org/Article.aspx?id=11488

Rob Stein, The Washington Post (December 21, 2007), *U.S.
Fertility Rate Hits 35-Year High, Stabilizing Population*
http://www.washingtonpost.com/wp-
dyn/content/article/2007/12/20/AR2007122002725.html

Wikipedia, RFID Technology (2008)
http://en.wikipedia.org/wiki/RFID

Wikipedia, Celtic Tiger (2008)
http://en.wikipedia.org/wiki/Celtic_Tiger

Financial Post (December 05, 2008), *Saskatchewan sees
strong job growth*
http://www.financialpost.com/story.html?id=1037083

Neil Howe and Richard Jackson, The Detroit News
(January 8, 2009) *Golden years start to look grim*
http://detnews.com/apps/pbcs.dll/article?AID=/20090108/
OPINION01/901080348

Origins analysis with DNA genealogy, iGena
http://www.igenea.com/index.php?c=900

Claudio Zucchelli & Dag Kirsebom, *Hard Landing*,
Beautiful People OÜ (2008)
www.hardlanding.ee

Stephanie Nebehay, *Swiss chocolate sales scale
Matterhorn heights*, Reuters (February 8, 2008)
http://uk.reuters.com/article/lifestyleMolt/idUKL08342207
20080208?pageNumber=1&virtualBrandChannel=0

Seth Sherwood, The New York Times (January 22, 2006)
Party Capital of the Year: Tallinn, Estonia
http://travel.nytimes.com/2006/01/22/travel/22tallinn.html

Medicine:

American Association of Medical Colleges (2008) *Tuition
and Student Fees Reports*
http://services.aamc.org/tsfreports/select.cfm?year_of_stud
y=2009

American Association of Medical Colleges (2008) *FACTS -
Applicants, Matriculants, Graduates, and Residency
Applicants* http://www.aamc.org/data/facts/start.htm

Tamara Vlastelica Bakic, Deloitte (2008), *60 billion annual
profits from medical tourism*
http://www.deloitte.com/dtt/press_release/0,1014,cid%253
D226608,00.html

Steve Roman, Baltic Times (Jan 18, 2006), *Estonia faces
medical 'brain drain'*
http://www.baltictimes.com/news/articles/14443/

Mayo Clinic (2008), *History of the Mayo Clinic*
http://www.diavlos.gr/orto96/ortowww/historym.htm

Coal vs. Nuclear

Mara Hvistendahl, Scientific American (December 13,
2007), *Coal Ash Is More Radioactive than Nuclear Waste*
http://www.sciam.com/article.cfm?id=coal-ash-is-more-
radioactive-than-nuclear-waste

Neil M. Cabreza, University of California, Berkley,
Department of Nuclear Engineering: *Nuclear Power VS.
Other Sources of Power*
http://www.nuc.berkeley.edu/thyd/ne161/ncabreza/sources.
html

The Virtual Nuclear Tourist (2006), *Why use Nuclear
Power?*
http://www.nucleartourist.com/basics/reasons1.htm

Dr. Phillip J. Finck, Argonne National Laboratory (2005)
Congressional Hearing on Nuclear Fuel Reprocessing
http://www.anl.gov/Media_Center/News/2005/testimony05
0616.html

Entergy Corporation (2008), *Answers on Nuclear Power
and Indian Point*
http://www.safesecurevital.org/nuclear-power-faqs/

Cook Energy Information Center (2008),
http://www.cookinfo.com/emer/rads.htm

World Nuclear Association (August 2008), *Waste Management in the Nuclear Fuel Cycle*
http://www.world-nuclear.org/info/inf04.html

Randall Parker, The Future Pundit (June 22,2006) *Thorium Nuclear Reactor Designs Advancing*
http://www.futurepundit.com/archives/003536.html

Military & Defence

BBC (September 29, 2006) *The Graeco-Persian Wars: The Battle of Thermopylae*
http://www.bbc.co.uk/dna/h2g2/A12889146

Dmitry Sidorov, Kommersant (April 10, 2008) *Russian Army Fails to Impress Americans*
http://www.kommersant.com/p878513/Conference_on_Russian_military_reform_held_in_America/

Wikipedia (2008), *The Military of Switzerland*
http://en.wikipedia.org/wiki/Military_of_Switzerland

US Department of State, Bureau of European and Eurasian Affairs (July 2008) *Background Note: Russia*
http://www.state.gov/r/pa/ei/bgn/3183.htm

Dave Shaver, Post-Bulletin (December 11, 2008) *Russia is not ready to fight a major war*
http://www.postbulletin.com/newsmanager/templates/localnews_story.asp?z=12&a=374770

Dmitry Solovyov, Reuters (February 13, 2008) *Bullied Russian soldier dies in hospital*

http://www.reuters.com/article/latestCrisis/idUSL13889482
Ben Aris, Telegraph (June 19, 2001) *Russian soldiers forced to dig in for their supper*
http://www.telegraph.co.uk/news/worldnews/europe/russia/1356416/Russian-soldiers-forced-to-dig-in-for-their-supper.html

Robert K. Maddock Jr. MD (1998) *The Finnish Winter War*
http://www.kaiku.com/winterwar.html and
http://www.kaiku.com/notcapitulate.html

Korn/Ferry International (2006), *Military Experience & CEOs: Is There a Link?*
www.kornferry.com/

Acknowledgements

Indre Grover, my wife

Derek Ewen, my friend in Saareemaa

All of my colleagues and friends in Estonia

About this Book

When this book was submitted for publication at two major Estonian business news organizations, I expected and received the following reactions:

This book is too short. My intention is to encourage people to think about their own lives and their future in a logical manner. I would like to encourage people to use deductive reasoning to arrive at their own conclusions. I could have filled this book up with facts, figures and statistics. They are helpful in supporting the main topic and I put them in where I felt they were needed. My intention for the reader is to see the forest from the trees. If people fixate on statistics and minutia they may miss the main idea of the book: multiple ideas interconnecting to form a synergetic solution where the whole is greater than the sum of the parts. The main idea is that change will come from within.

The author does not know Estonia or its situation: I have lived in Estonia for almost five years. Before that I visited Estonia in 1997 while in the US Navy and in 2000-2001 while I was living in Sweden. I came to live in Estonia in 2004 where I have been successful in real estate entrepreneurship, importing cars from the USA and selling them locally. I have been going the all the motions of life in Estonia that any ordinary Estonian goes through: paying taxes, taking a home loan, paying this loan, dealing with the various ministries, registering automobiles, getting insurance, going to doctors, buying groceries, cooking, paying the bills, going to the movies, notaries, festivals, sending mail etc. Moreover, I have not only visited and met face to face with people in Tallinn but also Lasname, Mustamae, Parnu, Sindi, Tartu, Voru, Vigale, Rapla, Narva, Kuressaare, Mustjala, Kivioli, Haapsalu, Panga Pank, Saue, and many more places throughout the Baltics.

By living here, conducting business, travelling about, holding a job, I have gained a great deal of insight into this nation, at least enough to write about it. Many criticize me that I didn't have the experience of going to Siberia or getting jailed by the Soviets. My answer to that is that neither have many of the young people living in Estonia today.

I believe Media choke points exist. Estonian is spoken by relatively few people worldwide; there are only a small amount of news publications in Estonia. Hence, the media is the gate keeper to those who only know Estonian. I watch TV here. The English channels such as CNN or BBC seldom talk about Estonia. The media and whoever controls them thru ad-revenue, public policy or by family connections can control the information flow. With limited sources, people can only develop their views with limited information. My conclusion is that foreigners residing in Estonia should publish and share their views more often so that the average Estonian can have complete information before taking a stance on an issue.

"That even any Estonian is not right person to tell what Estonia should do. It needs more than living in Estonia." Alexis de Tocqueville, a French political thinker and historian, wrote *Democracy in America* (1835) which highlighted the strengths and weaknesses of the United States. It is regarded as a classical account of the democratic system of the United States and has been used as an important reference in the USA and throughout the

world ever since. American's and many other western nations put high value on what outsiders say. Its incredible America was doing this within one generation from the time it gained its independence.

I always hear this tired phrase, "this is their country, and you have no right to tell them what to think." In my view, Estonia belongs to everyone who lives here. I am offering my view as a foreign national who lives and works in Estonia. A society is made up and influenced by all its inhabitants. Furthermore, the last time I checked, Estonia is a democracy which means it has freedom of speech and press. People both Estonian and foreigner should be encouraged to speak their mind. It will make life better for all in the long run if all the wheels of democracy are moving: press, voting, dissent, debate etc. The media owes its society different points of view.

It is preposterous to think that a society can develop in a vacuum and devoid of contact from the outside. In fact it's quite healthy to remain isolated from the world. The effects of inbreeding deplete the gene pool and leads to extinction.

Throughout History, mankind has been mixing it up: trade, marriage, exploration and alliances. Many foreigners have and companies have contributed to landscape in Estonia and have become figureheads and symbols of Estonian life.

In Saaremaa, once can find an Italian restaurant owned by an American. The locals will tell you its one of the best places to eat in Kuressaare. The landmarks in the Tallinn Old Town were built by Estonians, Danes, Russian and Germans. Favourite restaurants like Controvento, Café VS and Argentina are foreign owned and frequented by Estonians. The success of these businesses means that the foreigners have been doing a good job of listening to their clients, most of which are Estonians, and giving them what they want.

The foreigners living here have a vested interest in Estonia. They have come from far away, in some cases leaving very comfortable lifestyle, to conduct business, employ people and invest vast amounts of their time and money into this nation. It is only polite to hear their views as you would hear the views of anyone else who lives here.

The religion subject is irrelevant to Estonian Readers:
Religion has been an integral part to every society since human existence. In every society religion, politics and culture intertwine. It shapes our views, sense of morality and priorities in life. Estonia has a lot of churches, some of which are national symbols. Religion has always been relevant and will always continue to be relevant when discussing the state of the nation, its people and its future. Any attempt to stamp out or censor religion has always backfired and caused a nations demise. Church and state must be kept separate in government. Government must make neither favor nor suppress religion. However, it is unavoidable that religion helps shape governmental policy and ideals.

About the Author

Alexander Grover currently works in the Estonian financial industry as a marketing director. He has resided in Tallinn for almost five years and has a wife Indre who is from Vilnius, Lithuania. He enjoys going to the gym, cross country skiing, skating, skiing and watching *Animal Planet* shows. He is always trying to find relationships between scientific and engineering principles, nature and our daily lives.

He was born in Minnesota during the Nixon era as the son of Indian immigrants. His father was an engineer for Minnesota Mining and Manufacturing, better known as 3M and his mother was a pre-school teacher. His family later moved to suburban Chicago where he completed high school (secondary school) in 1989. In addition to graduating as an Illinois State Scholar, he competed in cross-country running and wrestling. He studied one year at the University of Southern California and later transferred to Kansas State University where he completed his Bachelors of Science in Nuclear Engineering in 1994. He was also on the Kansas State varsity rowing team, winning and placing in both state and regional competitions. He completed his MBA in Marketing from the University of Illinois at Chicago in 2005, a portion of which was done in Sao Paulo, Brazil.

His professional career started at Price Waterhouse (now known as Price Waterhouse Coopers) right out of college in the early 90's. Three months after joining PW later he decided that he needed more adventure and left this prestigious job for the US Navy where he served as an active duty commissioned officer for almost five years. Upon completion of service, he worked as an IT project manager for Ericsson in Sweden and later as a continuous improvement project manager (Six Sigma Black Belt) for Sears Holding Corporation.

Book website: TheNewEstonianGoldenAge.com

Elu on nii nagu sa selle kujundad...